For Louise —
a beautiful
soul whose
freindship.
I cherish!

With much love.

Richard

7/19/12

Theatre: Its Healing Role in Education

Theatre: Its Healing Role in Education

Richard Morse

VANTAGE PRESS
New York

Cover design by Kamren Charpentier

FIRST EDITION

Copyright © 2009 by Richard Morse

Published by Vantage Press, Inc.
419 Park Ave. South, New York, NY 10016

Manufactured in the United States of America
ISBN: 978-0-533-15867-6

Library of Congress Catalog Card No.: 2007905372

0 9 8 7 6 5 4 3 2 1

For Margie Hamlin and Bente Morse,

*Two sister angels, radiating hope, direction, and love
to the young people of this world*

Go forth, little book, from my halting pen, into the world of men and women of learning, knowledge, culture and research! ... Preach the gospel of happiness in childhood for those who will be the world's workers and fighters tomorrow.
— *Harriet Finlay Johnson*

All the arts combine in the theatre, décor, the dance, impersonation, effective speech, the song, pantomime, the projection of personality, the art of suppressing self, and even ill will, for the sake of unity of effort. Hundreds of other arts could be listed including the art of living together and the art of creative imagination. That is why the play can never be omitted from child education.
— *Hughes Mearns*

The Day of the Emancipation of Drawing has come, that of the teaching of Music has dawned, and I hope that of the teaching of Drama in schools is at hand.
— *Gavin Bolton*

CONTENTS

FOREWORD

I first knew Richard Morse through his performances with his Mime Theatre in New York City.

We saw each other occasionally after his theater closed, and then there was a period when I didn't see him at all, and I had no idea of what he was up to.

Many years later he came to see a play of mine and after the performance we talked and he told me he was writing a book which he would like me to read, and if I liked it he hoped I would write a foreword. From what he said (he always talks with great energy and enthusiasm), I thought it would have something to do with Mime, and his experiences performing in his theater in New York, and on tour here and abroad. The manuscript arrived and I looked at the title page and read in bold type: "Theatre: Its Healing Role in Education" which was a little intimidating to me, and I glanced at Part One and its chapters "Problems Facing Our Children," "The Story of Lucia Lopez, 'Gang Banger' from the Mean Streets of Piltsin," "Two Deaf Boys Find Their 'Voices'." "A Foiled Suicide, and an Entire School Year Turned Around," and I began to read.

I'm always apprehensive when reading a friend's work. What do you say if you don't like it? To say "I liked it" is to put it mildly. I found all three sections absorbing and very moving.

I have read it through three times and I'm always moved by these stories demonstrating what is possible, through love and dedication, and using various theater techniques, to make a healing difference in the lives of children and young people.

What Richard Morse has accomplished and what he assures us can be accomplished to ease the pain and frustration of the young is a wake up call to us all.

—Horton Foote
Pulitzer Prize winning playwright
Twice Academy Award Winner for Best Screenplay
Emmy Award Winning author for television

PREFACE

While attending Principia College, a small liberal arts college in the Midwest in the late 1940s, I was fortunate to study under a remarkable teacher, Mr. Frank Parker. (Plate 1) He saw the theatre in large terms connected with painting, sculpture and music. Before turning to teaching, Mr. Parker had performed internationally as a "diseur," or theatre performer who combines acting with mime and song. His teaching stimulated in me a wide exposure to art history as well as world theatre.

Throughout our theatre studies, Frank Parker conveyed yet another important theme: the potential of theatre to transform lives. We studied Molière, and relected on critic George Meredith's "Essay on Comedy," which underlined the themes of correction and change gracefully embedded in the comic master-pieces of the great French playwright.

Questions of healing and transformation remained dormant with me for many years, however, as I pursued a New York acting career that also included teaching acting and mime courses at the HB (Uta Hagen—Herbert Berghof) Studio in New York. In the summer of 1969, students in our mime classes insisted that we put our studies to the test through public performances. We were invited by the Carl Shapley school in Ridgefield, Connecticut, to take up residence to perform nightly for the community under a large green and white striped circus-style tent. The community had a great time with our work, and we were delighted.

Word of our work expanded, mostly from our classes, and in 1971 a remarkably talented woman, Pilar Garcia, and I, were invited to perform as the Richard Morse Mime Theatre, in the reper-

(Plate 1) Frank Parker: a legendary teacher. (Photo courtesy of Principia College Archives)

tory of the Cleveland Play House for the 1971–72 season. The visionary artistic director, Richard Oberlin, had the courage to gamble on this art form hardly known to the American public.* To our relief and delight the fall performance was a great success, calling for a second show in the spring called "Duet," which was even more successful with audiences and the press.

Feelings of triumph momentarily distracted me from thinking about the healing and transformational powers of theatre, until Producer Oberlin made another bold decision: to sponsor a special show for young people from inner city areas who would not otherwise have the opportunity to see live theatre. Oberlin scheduled a series of one-hour morning performances, and children were bussed into the Play House's Brooks Theatre from all corners of Cleveland.

Grateful letters from public school teachers began to reach us recounting the positive effects that theatre was producing in their classrooms, including how it was lifting student morale. One instructor recounted that days after seeing our show, her students were still walking through imaginary doors, scaling precarious mountainsides, and floating over Lake Erie buoyed by invisible balloons! This enterprising teacher decided to heed the *vox populi*, and voilà!—theatre became a newfound joy in the classroom.

In addition to testifying to a boost in morale, the teachers also exulted in the fact that a newfound sense of play identified the classroom as a much more happy place to be and the students were learning better. Nowadays we have many testimonies confirming this connection between the pleasure of learning and better grade scores. Here is just one from a 1995 study published by the National Endowment for the Arts in Washington:

---

*A woman called the box office to inquire what mime theatre was. When learning that she would be attending a performance of silent theatre, she suggested that, if there were no words, the theatre should really charge half price.

Vocabulary and reading comprehension were significantly im-proved for elementary students in the "Arts Alternatives" pro-gram in New Jersey. A strong connection between drama skills and literacy was found in this program, which involved role-playing, improvisational techniques and story writing activi-ties.*

In 1972 we returned to New York where our mime work con-tinued at The Billy Munk Theatre, a tiny 71-seat house three sto-ries above a bar on 45th Street and Second Avenue. The backstage area had no heat, and there were shivering nights when tempera-tures plummeted below freezing. During those evenings, two an-cient and courageous wall heaters puffed valiantly to warm bundled audiences. Yet nobody seemed to mind. New York thea-tre critics showed up, undaunted by the primitive conditions, and cheered us on with wonderfully favorable reviews. Our audience steadily expanded.

A children's theatre was soon added to the adult repertoire under the inventive direction of Rasa Allan. In 1974 our mime troupe moved to a more congenial theatre home (with heat!) at the St. John's church on Waverly Place in Greenwich Village. Satur-day morning mime classes for children were added, and once a month an original children's show was performed under the mas-terful guidance of Eric Berglund. The children not only performed their own pieces, but also helped to create their own sets and cos-tumes, thus acquiring a wide range of skills. The theatre was packed on these occasions as parents, among others, proudly cheered their children on. These proved to be very rich days in the life of the New York community.

*National Endowment for the Arts, *Eloquent Evidence, 5.*

At one matinee for one of our many special shows for deaf and mute children, an interesting event took place. At the height of the show's hilarity, a child broke out into speech for the first time. "He's speaking! He's speaking!" exclaimed his teacher, as the child was roundly embraced and encouraged to say more. There have been other similar incidents. Leading theatre-in-education teacher, Beth Murray, records one:

> *Apparently during a later drama session, the child actually spoke his first words and was whisked off to be seen by specialists and what have you: the drama had elicited a major breakthrough for the child. A remarkable moment to behold, no doubt.*[*]

We know that joy and laughter are liberators of the human spirit. Can they produce healing effects, such as loosening the tongue strings of a mute child? It would appear so.

Two strong facets of theatre are the focus of this book: theatre as a healing influence, and theatre as a learning tool. Actually, the two are inseparable. As students are freed from social snares of alienation, hopelessness and violence, they inevitably learn better; and as the joy of theatre is integrated into the curriculum, students begin to feel bonding, self-assurance and peace.

Today a long list of leading performing artists are looking beyond the footlights to discover satisfying ways to enrich their careers. Names such as Bono, Doris Day, Sigourney Weaver, Oprah Winfrey, Ashley Judd and Angelina Jolie come to mind. Oprah Winfrey states:

> *To whom much is given, much is expected. You can't live in the world, participate in all the benefits of the world, and not give*

*Murray, *Nowhere to Hide But Together*, 1998.

back. It goes against the laws of physics. If you don't give back, then what you have will be diminished.[*]

Many former college students write telling me that the experience of creating theatre with young people in the classroom and the community is proving to be a great source of inspiration in their lives. Some have committed themselves to this field with remarkably creative results.

The writer hopes that this book might lead others, within or without the theatre field, to discover this satisfaction.

*   *   *

WITH GREAT THANKS . . .

Though the list be incomplete, some acknowledgment of those who contributed directly or indirectly to this book is necessary.

First, I honor the memory of my college mentor, Mr. Frank Parker whose influence has shaped my vision of theatre to this day. His career is a constant reminder to me, and to many others, of what a vital role an inspired teacher can play in our lives.

I thank the enthusiastic students at the HB Studio who insisted that we put our classroom learning to the test through public performance.

Thanks to all the actors and technicians whose artistic and selfless devotion helped establish the Richard Morse Mime Theatre as a New York and world theatre company. These include: Pilar Garcia, Rasa Allan for her essential work in establishing us as a New York and International theatre company, the late David McGee, Tony Curry, Byam Stevens, Gjertine Johansen, Kristin

[*]*USA Today*, June 23, 2006, 2A.

Sakai, Barbara Knight, Lee Copenhaver, Charles Penn, Richard Hall, Miho, Shep Sobel, Peggy Imrie, Jack Gremli, Elsie Hoel, K.C. Schulberg, David Rosenberg, Gabe Barre, Philip Burton, Eric Berglund, Mark Keeler, Ken Michaelson, Tom Candela, Dianne Howarth, Michael Belanger, Jack Boyle, Sharon Fenwald, Ellen Polan, Leonore Bode, Anastasia Nicole, Ann Marie Hackett, Manuel Landrove, Robert Maiorano, Tamara Schrader, Elan Kozuk, James Uehling, Linda Allen, Tricia Paoluccio, Ian Wilder for outstanding support in every way; to Jim Shelly for invaluable technical help; and heartfelt thanks to David Brooks for remarkable design support and so much else.

Also, to Gigi Bolt then of the New York State Council; to the many critics who believed in our work and said so; to the Principia College administration who encouraged and supported this project of the book and its two DVDs; to Sue Fuller of the Principia College Library; to Charlotte Wallace and Karen Winder who contributed editing help.

A very special thanks to Paula Bradley whose eye to both the text and the DVD version of this book was absolutely indispensable.

Thanks to the generous support of Larry Charlston, Director of Video Production at Principia College. Equally to John Lyons head of Media Services at Principia College, and to John Tambuckle for his help with recording.

Overwhelming thanks here to Rick Dearborn, a true friend, for accomplishing the DVD version of this book.

Deepest thanks to my friend, Norman Anderson, who urged me to write this book and had the faith that I, a non-writer, could do it.

Forgive me if the passage of many years has caused me to neglect others. (Hopefully there will be a second edition!)

Finally, I can only attempt the impossible, in recognizing the help of my wife, Bente, who has been indescribably supportive in everything touching this project, from traveling the globe with me to making room in her busy career to establish herself as a video camera operator par excellence!

To all, my heartfelt love and deep thanks.

Note to the reader: Where applicable, DVD coverage is indicated in parentheses at the top of each chapter. Ex: (*DVD disc 1, section 3*).

Theatre: Its Healing
Role in Education

Part I

Helping Our Children

ONE

PROBLEMS FACING OUR CHILDREN

Adults are failing our children. Our smart, well-educated kids, even those in fine suburban schools, know everything about gender, race, human rights, and giving to charity, but they don't learn about inclusion and kindness. . . . If we want a society that does not discriminate, we cannot allow cruelty to run rampant in lunchrooms and at recess. The issue is not "not discriminating"; it is not even "not bullying." These are passive actions. . . . We must practice and model kindness and inclusion. Adults must challenge the assumption that cliques and rejection are part of human nature. Kids are born, then they learn to reject. Instead they can learn to include.

—Hannah Achtenberg Kinn*

Students no longer show enough love. Granted there are exceptions, but the majority of the student body seems not to care, because everyone looks out for themselves alone. Every student needs to feel love, care, respect and acceptance at school.
—High school student Allison Keeley**

> *Oh, God, oh, God, I feel such pain.*
> *My life is slipping down the drain.*
> *Oh, God, I need a helping hand.*

*Letter to the *New York Times,* March 13, 2001.
**Michener, "Students Blame Bullying," *St. Louis Post Dispatch*, August 29, 1999, B5.

3

On a March evening of 2005, I heard these words declaimed by a teenage detainee at the St. Louis City Juvenile Detention Center. The occasion was a performance evening of Hip-Hop poetry sponsored by the Saint Louis-based Prison Performing Arts (PPA) organization as part of a rehabilitation program. I can recall years ago first hearing similar words uttered by young people incarcerated in detention centers and prisons. In a system which seemed more interested in punishment than in transformation, I would often feel frustrated with a strong desire to help but not understanding what I could do. In many institutions, even one-on-one contact was difficult.

During the past ten years I realized that large segments of our society's children, though not incarcerated, are themselves prisoners of harsh social conditions, such as exclusion, poverty, and hopelessness which often evolve into frustration, anger and violence.

When I began my career, I would never have considered myself a "sociologist." I came to see, however, that the activity of theatre contained its own "sociology" and could deliver these young people from these harrowing social conditions and transform lives. My theatrical preoccupations, until then focused on a personal career, gradually evolved to include effecting change with these young people and building hope. Over the years I met many remarkable people pursuing the same path. Many of their stories form the substance of this book.

As I pursued questions of individual transformation, I was struck by what history had to teach us. For example, our shamanic ancestors, dating from the Stone Age, perceived inclusion as the key to healing. For them, healing involved a shape, and that was the circle. When a member of the community was ailing, either physically or mentally, this individual was considered to have wandered outside the circle of the clan. It was at this point that the designated healer of the tribe, known as the shaman, conducted

4

strenuous exercises, supported by the community, to return the patient to *within* this circle. When this was accomplished and clan connection re-established, the healing took place.

Our ancestors obviously understood the dangers produced through a loss of connection. When we consider the widespread alienation faced by today's young people—young from their parents, young from teachers, and young from the young—we can further appreciate their wisdom. The need for inclusion could be said to be the central theme of this book. We will see in the following pages how our young people are crying out for these bonds of connection, even while in the process of attempting to destroy them. It is interesting that in questioning many young people on the value of a theatre program, by far the word most often uttered was "family."

Before embarking on an exploration of the theatre as a socializing and a learning tool, we might do well to remind ourselves of conditions faced by many of our schoolchildren on a daily basis. Some, whether familiar with these factors or not, may find this an upsetting prelude to our story. I hope that the reader will come to see, however, that this somber backdrop is developed only to enhance the brighter colors of hope to emerge in the pages that follow.

*   *   *

On April 20, 1999, at Columbine High School in Littleton, Colorado, two students opened fire with attack weapons and killed twelve fellow classmates and a teacher, before taking their own lives. Our nation and the world were stunned. Nationwide strong security measures were quickly put in place, including stiffer penalties, more patrolling police, ubiquitous locks, and the reporting of all suspicious behavior. One young boy was sent to the principal's office for resting his head on his arm over his desk.

Society suddenly wanted to know what was going wrong

5

with our children. Inquiries and studies probed these questions with an urgency that suggested teenage violence was something new. Yet, long before Columbine a rising frequency in high school violence had been reported by highly visible and official publications all over the United States.

A 1991 report by Bernardino Dohrn of Northwestern University School of Law was one of many alerting society in America to the cresting of teen homicides.

Between 1984 and 1994, youth homicide skyrocketed. The number of young people charged with killing another young person increased by 144 percent. 75 percent of all child murders in the industrialized world now take place in the United States. And United States youngsters are twice as likely to commit suicide.[*]

In another tragic assault on March 21, 2005, the worst since Columbine, a young student of the Red Lake Reservation of Native American Indians in Red Lake, Minnesota, also went on a shooting rampage in which ten lives including his own were lost. In both Columbine and Red Lake, there were similar circumstances surrounding the experiences of the perpetrators. In both instances an alienation from parents, fellow students and school authorities was strongly in evidence. For one thing, Jeff Weise, the perpetrator at Red Lake, as Dylan Klebold and Eric Harris at Columbine, had all been unmercifully teased and derided by fellow students. All three had taken to wearing long black trench coats emphasizing their hurt and rage. The backgrounds of the three assailants shared similar factors: records of parental neglect, abuse, and unchecked bullying in the schools on the parts of teachers and school officials. Weise had developed a website when confined to his home by school authorities. On one of the discovered mes-

*Dohrn, *Youth Violence*, 2.

sages, he declared that his mother "would hit me with anything she could get her hands on," and "would tell me I was a mistake and she would say so many things that it's hard to deal with them or think of them without crying."[*]

Despite all precautions of police surveillance, locks and hidden cameras, fatal shootings continue to occur in frightening frequency in all parts of America. The most horrible of these in recent times was the mass killing of thirty-two students and teachers at Virginia Polytechnic Institute on April 16, 2007, when a young man, also manifesting the same symptoms of isolation and frustration as Klebold, Harris and Weise, committed these killings in sudden rage. The questions as to the causes of these massacres persist, even though the symptoms of bullying and isolation continue to appear.

"Are some children just bad by nature, or are there identifiable causes?" are questions often pondered. On this point the controversy still smolders. *New York Times* staff writer, David Brooks, states in a May 5, 2004 column: "My instinct is that Dylan Klebold was a self-initiating moral agent who made his choices and should be condemned for them. Neither his school nor his parents determined his behavior." This is a shocking statement in view of what is known about Klebold, Harris and the prevalent atmosphere at Columbine High School in 2002, and also at Red Lake in 2005. It produced two letters of rebuttal in the May 18, 2004 edition of *The New York Times*. The first, authored by Thomas W. Clark, a research associate at *Health and Addictions Research,* quotes the Brooks theory cited above, and then adds:

Certainly Dylan Klebold's choices are condemnable, but they were not self-initiated . . . By claiming that moral agency is mysteriously self-constructed, Mr. Brooks short-circuits the investiga-

*[*New York Times,* March 24, 2005. (A14)

tion of what drove Dylan Klebold to murder and suicide and makes prevention of similar horrors more difficult. [*]

A letter on the same page by Stuart Green, Director of *New Jersey Coalition for Bullying Awareness and Prevention,* is more specific in detailing causes:

David Brooks, while right to be supportive of Dylan Klebold's parents ("Columbine parents of a Killer" column, May 15), should not dismiss the importance of the school as a major factor in the killings. Dylan Klebold was a bullied child, attending a school in which bullying was not being adequately addressed. Bullied children suffer tremendously, cannot end the bullying by themselves, and occasionally kill themselves or, rarely, others.

Adults are capable of effectively addressing bullying, but most continue not to do so. The "self-initiating moral agent who made his choices and should be condemned for them" is not only Dylan Klebold, It is also the adults in charge of his school.

Blaming the child alone won't solve the problem and the problem needs to be solved. [**]

A high incidence of intimidation, bullying and social ostracism was noted by Columbine's own students. A close friend of Dylan Klebold was quoted in a *New York Times* interview:

Dylan Klebold was one of my best friends. And when I hung out with him, there was just something that happened. I mean, whether they were wearing jeans and T-shirt, or whether they were wearing their black trench coats, people would give them looks. Just like, "You don't belong here, would you leave?" Let's block out

*Clark, Thomas, Letter to *The New York Times.* May 18, 2004, A24.
**Green, Stuart, Letter . . . , A24.

*last week when I say this—they hadn't done anything physically
wrong to people. I mean, they dressed different. So?*

*They wore black. So what? It's just, they were hated and so
they hated back. They hated back.*[*]

The divisive tides of intolerance are sad features of our public
schools. In an article entitled "The Outsiders," high school student
Alvin Toffer bears witness to their presence:

*It (Columbine) certainly didn't happen because of the lack of a
school committee. Their problem was, they (Harris and Klebold)
weren't accepted, and that's the way that our society is. There are
always people that are going to be cast out and people that are
cast in.*[**]

High school student Amanda Austerman of St. Louis not
only concurs with Toffer, but adds a sad indictment of her teachers.

*One of my best friends was made fun of by a teacher. This teacher
would make comments in front of the entire class about my friend,
leaving all the students laughing at her. A role model like this
makes all of the other students think this kind of behavior is appropriate, but it's not. . . . Have you ever been called a freak or a
snob? Have you ever been bullied, made fun of, or beaten up because someone didn't like you for being different? Nearly all high
school students experience at least one of these things during high
school. What most people don't realize is that these are very serious issues. The people who don't take these issues seriously are,*

[*]McFadden, Robert D. *New York Times,* April 30, 1999, *Terror in Littleton: Some Answers,
More Questions: Columbine Students Talk of the Disaster and Life.* (1)

[**]Also discovered on Weise's internet communication: "I have friends, but I'm basically a
loner. Inside a group of loners, I'm excluded from anything and everything they do. I'm
never invited." *New York Times,* March 24, 2005. (A14)

most of the time, the people who promote them . . . Bullies harass people because they are different from them. This can be life-damaging. Harassing someone for long periods of time causes anger to build inside of this person. When one decides enough is enough, boom! The next school shooting is here.[*]

To indicate the magnitude of this problem, America's schools declared March 7–13, 2004 as official *"National No Name Calling Week."* Problems of humiliation and bullying were the subject of national coverage in the press and other media. On May 5, 2004, National Public Radio broadcast an extensive examination of the subject. Agonized parents whose children had been victims of these cruel practices phoned in from all corners of the United States. Many of the calls confirmed the report of high school student, Amanda Austermann—that our teachers were doing little to intervene in attempting to curb these abusive practices.

Current statistics on child abuse in America are staggering. According to the 2005 report from the U.S. Department of Health and Human Services, in FFY (Federal Fiscal Year) 2005:

An estimated 899,000 children in 50 States, the District of Columbia and Puerto Rico were determined to be victims of abuse and neglect.

Nationally, 62.8 percent of child victims experienced neglect, 16.6 were physically abused, 9.3 percent were sexually abused, and 7.1 percent were emotionally or psychologically maltreated.[**]

Many sociologists and other observers of child behavior state that abuse does not simply "appear" in the life of a child. Its causes

[*]Testimony of Amanda Austerman "Students blame bullying," *The St. Louis Post Dispatch,* August 29, 1999. B-1

[**]*Child Maltreatment 2005*, a report of the U.S. Department of Health and Human Services. iii

lie within the milieu of family, relatives, and other children. It is part of a behavior which is not *accidental*, but *cyclical* in nature.

Principal Michael Dorso of the Baltimore school system commented in a 1994 report:

> *Children are not born or raised to be "disruptive youth." They often become wounded by the harsh realities of their family's and their own environments—abuse, neglect, poverty, addictions, learning disabilities, crime and violence. Children act according to what they see and live every day.*[*]

Veteran social worker Connie Burnett, who has served for twelve years with the St. Ann Habilitation Center and Family First Agency in St. Louis, has spent years investigating cases of child abuse. In an interview Burnett described harrowing stories of visits to homes where abuse was a horrible factor.

> *In one family of five children with an absent father in which I had to intervene, I observed a daughter with fifty scars on her body from beatings with an electrical cord from the mother. I worked with this family for three months. One night she opened up to me and said that she was confused and frustrated as to why we (the agency) were called in because she said that she had also been beaten like this by* her *parents. "This is the way my parents taught me respect," she exclaimed, "and now you come in and tell me what I'm doing is wrong."*[**]

The late Senator Daniel Patrick Moynihan, a perceptive critic writing on the American family, states:

*Report under the supervision of The Honorable William Donald Schaefer, Governor of Maryland: State House, Annapolis, Md. 1994. (10)

**Interview with social worker Connie Burnett, June 16, 2001.

11

We talk about the drug crisis, the education crisis and the problems of teen pregnancy and juvenile crime. But all these ills trace back predominantly to one source: broken families.[*]

However, broken families are not the fault of children, nor can children do much about them. For children to grow with any degree of normalcy, what is known as a "safe place" is needed. This means a milieu free from all kinds of abuse, physical, mental and intellectual.[**] Many feel these conditions can't be found in our troubled society. When the question, "Are our schools safe places in which to learn?" was posed to over 1000 students and parents across America for a 1997 Metropolitan Life Report, the response showed that: 48% of the parents and 23% of the students believed that "Teachers cannot effectively teach their students because of the threat of violence."[***]

Jocelynne James, a director of the Sesame School of Drama Therapy attached to London's Central School, told me in a London interview:

It is a miracle that education of any sort can take place at all. They (our abused children) come to me as casualties of education, as it is taught. They expect to be attacked, assaulted. <u>When they come, this is what they expect.</u> *I'm amazed that they get here! There is great resilience in them and in the arts. They have become marginalized by the national curriculum. Then we see them blos-*

*Moynihan, Daniel Patrick. 1996. (149–150)

**At a session of the 1997 Alliance of Theatre in Higher Education conference, educator Karen Erickson made the distinction of these 3 categories of abuse: the physical, where there is the threat of violence; mental, where there is the factor of degradation through prejudice; and intellectual abuse which tends to belittle the student for her/his lack of knowledge or scholastic abilities.

***Louis Harris and Associates. *The Metropolitan Life Survey of The American Teacher, 1994: Violence in America's Public Schools.* 1994. (147)

som and explode into being within the field of drama therapy."
(emphasis of Ms. James).

"Why the name, 'Sesame?' " I asked. Jocelynne replied:

The term 'Sesame' refers to the treasure that is universally found within each child. The task I and my associates face is to call forth this treasure. This is achieved in theatre-oriented practice and exercises. The approach employs the creative methods we must be prepared to utilize, often not found in textbooks of teacher education, in helping these damaged children back to a place of supportive identity which seems to be as much of a problem in London as it does in any major industrialized city. [*]

Many now concur with Jocelynne James that the exercise of theatre has the potential to provide a safe place where feelings of growth, connection and bonding can be established. A multitude of troubled young people who have entered the inclusive and sheltering refuge of a theatre program, even briefly, have seen their lives changed dramatically.

In considering our tasks in working with our children, I know of no more helpful and relevant words with which to close this chapter than the observation of anthropologist and author, Ashley Montagu. In 1950 Montagu wrote an important book, *On Being Human,* which concerns itself with the true nature of humankind. It is Montagu's contention that a false view has been thrust upon us through the images that surround us in daily life, bad psychology, or a misunderstanding of Darwin. In these days a Darwinian view which sees humankind as inescapably competitive, destructive and evil is widely accepted. But, Montagu insists that this viewpoint must be challenged. His book is also a reflection on the

*Jocelynne James, interview with author, London, Oct. 28, 1997.

13

question pondered by Principal Michael Dorso earlier in this chapter, and that is whether destructive tendencies are inherited or acquired. Montagu's response to this question is emphatic:

> *If we would seek for one word which describes society better than any other, that word is co-operation. . . . The impulses toward co-operative behavior are already present with him (the child) at birth, and all they require is cultivation. There is not a shred of evidence that man is born with "hostile" or "evil" impulses which must be watched and disciplined. Discipline is necessary, but it is the discipline of love, not of frustration, which they require.*
>
> *Love is the active state which is learned by the infant, and it is a state which is developed in dependency, and that is the pattern of love which is maintained throughout the life of the person. . . . Man is related to himself only in so far as he is related to others. To love is to relate oneself to others.*
>
> *The answer to our first question, "What is the nature of life?" can be expressed in one word, co-operation—the interaction between organisms for mutual support in such a way as to confer survival benefits upon each other. Another word for the same thing, as we shall see in the pages which follow, is love. Without co-operation, without love, it is not possible to live—at best, it's possible only to exist.*[*]

Truly, what greater gift can we provide for our young people than in conveying a proper estimation of who they are? Certainly a vision of their true natures and capacities forms the underpinning of all else.

*Montagu, Ashley, *On Being Human,* 1950. (145–147)

TWO

THE STORY OF LUCIA LOPEZ, FORMER "GANG BANGER" OF THE MEAN STREETS OF PILTSIN

This story demonstrates the kind of blossoming that can occur when our troubled children come upon the atmosphere of a "safe place." I heard this story on the National Public Radio program *This American Life* broadcast live from the stage of New York City's Town Hall on December 18, 1998. In this interview, entitled "What are You Looking At?", host Ira Glass was interviewing Lucia Lopez, an eighteen-year-old high school student from the rough slum district of Chicago known as Piltsin. Here is an excerpt from the NPR segment:

Ira: Back when she entered public school, like a lot of kids from her neighborhood, Lucia didn't speak English, Lucia didn't do well. As she got older, she found herself getting mad at the other kids, fighting all the time.

Lucia: I could not get a decent night's sleep, ever. I had to go to school with this image in my head, like, you know, I see my mom getting bashed into the wall, and I think that's what turned me into a very violent kid, . . . You know, like, just seeing other kids being happy was very . . . tough to me . . . because why can't I have fun like that? . . . . Why can't I live like that? . . . Why? . . . Why is it so difficult? . . . I was really bad. I was very bad with teachers. . . . If a

15

teacher was to even tell me, "Lucia, you have to be quiet," or whatever, I took that as an attack. I was . . . well if they're gonna' attack me, I should attack first . . . There was times like I might just be throwing chairs . . . whatever . . . you name it. . . . Since I was a little girl growing up I never, never had an o.k. day. . . . Do you understand me? . . . never had anything like . . . you know, . . . it's goin' to be cool today . . . It's gonna' be o.k. . . . You not goin' to hear one of your friend's dead and you're not goin' to hear anybody in your house beating up your mom. You're not gonna' hear that. . . . It's just gonna' be o.k. . . . it's just one of the things that . . . I just went through a whole different world.

I: A theatre group was brought to Lucia's attention at the Casa Atzlan in Piltsin, a deprived area of suburban Chicago, and she started work with the director, Meade Palidofsky. To hear Lucia tell it, she never met kids like the ones in the theatre group. Kids were strong and independent, but they weren't in the gang. And at first they were literally incomprehensible. The way they goofed around with each other, the way they talked with each other. She'd just watch them. Trying to understand why they acted the way they did. Why were they so happy all the time?

L: I just started seeing . . . like . . . these kids weren't in gangs. You know, they, they just had to tell me their lives . . . like I had one tellin' me, "You know . . . you don' have to be here . You don' have to do this and that" . . .

I: You mean the MTW (Music Theater Workshop) kids saying, "You don't have to be in the gang?"

L: Yeah! . . . And just to hear somebody from my age tell me that. You know that would really trip me out. I was like "Wow!" That was persons my age and they're thinking like this? . . . Ya' know . . . why can't I . . . why don' I think like that? . . . I thought, "what's wrong with me?" . . .

16

I: They were the only people in her life who were urging her to change, to quit the gang. Everybody else in her life was either in the gang or close to it. And essential to this whole change that Lucia had to go through was, "What are you looking at? . . . Is it o.k. for somebody to just look at you, without it turning into some kind of fight?" And for a long time, even in the theatre group, she struggled and she just thought "No."

L: And if you looked at me in any way, no matter how you looked at me, man you'll be dealt with.

I: You know what was so weird was that you got out of the whole thing by putting yourself in a position where you're on stage and people are looking at you!

L: (laughing) Yeah! Exactly! (large Town Hall audience bursts into laughter). I was really like . . . like . . . "Wow, I better get used to it!" . . . I was thinking like, "I can't be attacking everybody who's looking at me doin' the play." (outburst of laughter)

I: Should you be standing on stage, in a play, like in a costume, and you look out and you see all the other people looking at you, and going through your mind would be:

L: Yeah, like, "What the hell you lookin' at?! (burst of laughter from audience) . . . OOO, what's their problem?" Whatever. . . . And just like "What are they looking at me for?" It's like, "Man, should I tell them something? Should I go on the mike and say, 'Do youse all have a problem?' " (laughter) Should I be attacking? . . . That was what was going through my mind.

I: I also asked Lucia if it mattered that this was an arts group that she was in, that they were doing a play. Wouldn't she have changed if she had fallen in with any group of kids that she had liked, who were not in gangs, that she could get to know this way, and she said, "Absolutely not!" She said part of what helped her

17

change so much, part of what had made her quit the gang and go to school had specifically to do with the fact that it was a play. It was art, doing what art does, if you're lucky, which is: change you.

L: I think the play did a lot. The play itself could . . . like I said, since it was part of my life story and stuff and playing it and doing it over and over it was like . . . like one of the things was just letting it go. You could just . . . like I said, . . . the whole drama skit . . . the whole life was just like on paper. . . . Just let it fly away . . . whatever. . . . Let it be thrown in the garbage . . . just, you know . . . it happened . . . but just . . .

I: You had to live on.

L: You had to . . . live on . . . just live on . . . then peace, finally . . . so that's one of the good things . . . (quietly) . . . to feel peace . . . peace . . . and going to sleep better . . .

(End of excerpt)

I was so struck by Lucia's story that I felt that I must seek her out, both to confirm what I had heard and also to know how things were going with her some months later.

Piltsin is an impoverished neighborhood of Chicago. For two hours on a warm spring afternoon in 1999 I had been trying to maintain equilibrium over unevenly cracked sidewalks in seeking Lucia. I had knocked on three doors, only to discover that the Lopez family was continually ahead of me. I later learned that these changes of address were necessitated by the need to avoid an alcoholic stepfather who had been abusing Lucia and her mother over a period of twelve years.

After a third fruitless attempt, I sat, hot and exhausted, on a low stone wall. A fireman sitting casually outside his firehouse across the street noticed my perplexity and waved to me. I crossed the street and explained to this congenial gentleman that I was on a search for the Lopez family. "Wait," he said. He arose, and from an old wooden desk drawer pulled out a crumpled map. "Bueno, bueno," he muttered unfolding well-worn pages. "Now thees ees where you are. . . . Now thees," he drawled slowly, "thees is *where you wan' go.* The Lopez family leeve *ere.*" A pause, then, taking a stubby pencil from behind his ear, "Thees is the house, number 514 on Trumbull. Hokay?"

"Sí, sí, O.K. Muchas gracias!"

We shook hands and I departed, grateful that I still had a chance to find the elusive Lucia Lopez before dark. Fifteen minutes later, west by two avenues and north by five blocks, I finally came to 514 Trumbull. But the front door was boarded up. As I stepped back, I noticed a side door on this dilapidated wooden house that looked as if it had not been opened for many months. I made my way through a creaky iron gate and crossed a short flagstone path overgrown with stubby grass to a three step entrance. I could hear a squawking parrot and a child's voice within. I tapped on the door, expecting someone like Marjorie Main to poke her head through. No one answered. I knocked again, and heard a young child's voice, *"Mama! Mama! Hay alguien."* ("Mama! Someone's here.") Slowly the door opened a few inches and the head of a small grey-haired woman was silhouetted against the glare of an exposed light bulb within.

"Buenas dias, señora. Por favor, busco Lucia Lopez. Está en casa?" ("Good day, *señora*. Please, I am looking for Lucia Lopez. Is she at home?")

Pause, then, *"Quien está?"* ("Who are you?") she asked warily.

"Soy Ricardo Morse, amigo de la Señora Meade Palidofsky." (I am a friend of Meade Palidofsky, Richard Morse).

Pause.

Then, *"Sí. Ah, sí! . . . Momentito, por favor.* ("Just a moment please.") Lucia! . . . Lucia!"

The door opened wider, and a lovely girl in her late teens appeared. I had trouble imagining her as the "gang banger" of the Ira Glass interview. She opened the door wider and beckoned me in. I entered a dark living room furnished with a patched imitation leather sofa, several wooden chairs in varying styles and stages of harsh wear, and a small dining table of faded yellow wood. An observing parrot swung casually from a thin wire cage above.

Lucia offered to make me lunch. In a matter of minutes, and almost as if she had been expecting me, we were enjoying a plate of black beans with onions, a mixed salad and a strong Bustelo coffee filtered through a dark, stained sock. A fascinated mother, two occasionally gurgling infants, and the parrot looked on curiously in the fading light of day.

The following remarks are from my own personal encounter with Lucia:

R: I heard your remarkable story on "This American Life." Tell me something about the violent life you led.

L: Like I said I was growing up in a violent home . . . a violent household . . . I had to go to sleep every single night . . . well not actually go to sleep because I knew there was stuff . . . I would look at my stepfather who would hit my mother every single day. . . . So I grew up seeing it. I grew up seeing it from the small age when my mother got me which was two years old to when I was sixteen . . . sixteen, seventeen. . . . I thought, "that's how life is. That's what you got to deal with."

R: Do you think that seeing all this turned you into violence?

L: When you see somebody older who you think you respect is a violent person then you think that this sort of act is O.K. for you to do. If they're doing it, why can't you do it? . . . I think that's how I was brought up . . . seeing that every day . . . and I thought that was O.K. for me to do that. . . . I guess that's how it starts.

R: Lucia, you seem to be strong. Do you see hope for yourself now?

L: Of course, of course! . . . Or else I would have just been doing the same thing. Getting myself into problems, not accepting people, not letting nobody touch me, not letting nobody face me.

R: You said that theatre played an important part in changing your life. What did it do?

L: Well, like I said, it helped me cope with other people and to accept a lot of differences . . . it helped me see that there was another world out there from what I was looking at. . . . It really helped me out to progress in life. Actually, and like I said, I was really playing out my life experience which I let out when I was doing the play. I knew I wasn't letting it all go. But it was worth doing the play so many times.

R: What might have happened, do you think, if you hadn't done the play and hadn't been in the theatre program?

L: Well, I just would have been living my former life . . . as a gang banger.

R: A gang banger? What did you do there?

L: Well, I mean, it was like beating up on other kids.

R: Was the theatre work an important step in this?

L: It changed me a lot!

R: Would you think it might be good if other children had theatre in their classes?

L: Of course. You see a lotta' kids think that they don't have hope. We're brought up thinking that way.

R: Who tells you that?

L: Sometimes teachers. They don't really involve with you. Teachers are like "you have to know this, and you have to know that," but at the same time they see that a lot of kids have problems. But they don't say, "You're a good kid. You're a good kid. Do what you have to do. Don't worry what they tell you." . . . It's like most teachers just have to do a job and then get out.

R: And what you would like is more help from the teachers?

L: (emphatically) Oh, it'd be wonderful! *If a teacher was to tell me, . . . you know, this is your teacher, an' obviously when you're a little kid, . . . well, this is a smart lady . . . because she is a teacher. . . . When you see somebody who has that name, as being your teacher and somebody you have to respect tell you you're . . .* you're a good kid . . . ya' know it doesn't matter where you came from . . . you're a good kid, you know . . . *and you know what . . . you could be . . .* you could be much better than who you are. You could do whatever you want . . . you know whatever you want to get to . . . you could just <u>do</u> it . . . *and . . . I just wish there were more things like that. . . . It would be wonderful! . . . I don't know whether they get tired of working with kids like us . . . a lot of times we're very wild . . . I'm not sure if they get tired of that, but you know, they just don't bring that much hope . . . What I see is a lot of separation.*

R: Separation? Because you don't feel included?

L: Exactly.

R: Lucia, what do you think is the most important thing we can do for our children?

L: The most important thing? . . . Accepting them . . .

R: That's a big thing, isn't it?

L: If you see a bad kid, don't always push him to the side . . . don't always put him to the back of the classroom? Put him in the front of the classroom, put him with you. If they want to be bad, let them be bad in front of you . . . include *him to be bad with the whole class. . . . They have all that energy . . . let them use that energy.*[*]

I recall feeling that Lucia should be mentoring teachers.

Epilogue: Seven years later. April 9, 2006

Since 1999 Lucia had made two more trips to New York City to appear on the MTV television show, *Stop the Violence.* Host Joel Shumaker had heard of her story, and now it was inspiring many young people across America.

It is seven years later and Lucia is established at a new address in Chicago. Meade Palidofsky informed me that she had her own apartment, and provided me with her phone number. I called to find out what had happened in these years.

She told me she had earned a certificate as a Nurse's Aide and is awaiting the formal certification as a Nurse's Assistant. She works with the elderly, but also has occasion to counsel young people who are struggling, as she was, with violence. She says that talking with others makes them feel better, and that's what she enjoys doing. I asked her about personal changes that had taken place.

*Interview with Lucia Lopez, April 12, 1999.

23

L: A lot of personal change. I had to become more sociable. I learned what theatre was and what it can do.

R: Anything else?

L: Oh, my God, I learned that people really care. . . . Meade (Palidofsky) really struggled with me. I know that I wasn't doing good. But she gave me a chance.

R: What has giving you a chance meant?

L: Now I have a chance to talk to other people. People in trouble. I can tell them that this is only half of what there is. There is a lot more out there. . . . (pause) . . . I . . . I learned not to be afraid of things. That's what the theatre taught me. It gave me that self-esteem.

Lucia occasionally encounters her stepfather in the neighborhood. He was shocked to hear her on the radio. He now has a new respect for Lucia, her mother and her siblings, and there has been no recurrence of family abuse. Lucia's attitude is, as she expressed it to me: "I forgive you, but you're not going to hurt me any more."

She adds, "He even sends my mother a little money from time to time."*

*Telephone interview with Lucia Lopez, August 14, 2006.

24

THREE

TWO DEAF BOYS AND HOW THEY FOUND THEIR "VOICES"

Han's Story

"At the heart of his rehabilitation was the experience of performing theatre."

—*Lisa Agogliati*

When I met Han in the summer of 1997, he was a fifteen-year-old deaf Korean boy. He had emigrated to America with his mother when he was twelve. After spending some months in Chicago and finding no means of subsistence, mother and son, both refugees, moved to Bethesda, Maryland. The mother was seeking employment but found little success; her most important goal was to see to her son's education.

In 1995 she enrolled him in the eleventh grade at Bethesda's Rockville High School. Han's mother had learned that Rockville included a mainstream program for deaf students. It was here that Han met Lisa Agogliati, an instructor at the Bethesda Academy of the Performing Arts (BAPA) who also taught theatre at Rockville High.

BAPA works together productively with the Montgomery County Public School System, including Rockville High, to provide a theatre program to over 150 children who are deaf or hard of hearing. This organization also conducts the "Deaf Access Program" which emphasizes theatre activity for its students as part of their socialization process.

The day Han arrived an audition was about to take place for the theatre program of "The Snow Queen." Han won a role and suddenly found himself in an acting company of fourteen high school actors, half of which were deaf and half hearing.

Though he enjoyed the experience, Han still felt lonely in his new environment and had considerable trouble socializing. According to Lisa, a master of sign language, "He was still adjusting to yet another transition in his life—and he did not always seem happy. He would share with me details about his Korean culture through sign language and I tried to support and encourage him to share this part of his background with the Deaf Access 'family.' "[*]

Later that year, in February of 1996, Lisa was conducting her annual program called "Creative Arts Residency," at the high school attended by Han. The curriculum included eight weeks of Improvisation, Basic Acting, and Sign Language Poetry. Lisa helped Han to understand basic English through working with haiku poems. Lisa described what followed:

"He was hesitant at first, but soon started reading through poems I had brought in—along with the suggestion of working with original poems written by students—and he selected a haiku piece, which he performed.

> *"One lone pine tree*
> *growing in the hollow—*
> *And I thought*
> *I was the only one*
> *without a friend."*

How interesting a choice he made! It seemed to reflect the many emotions he may have been feeling at the time. We talked about the

*Lisa Agogliati interview, August 13, 1997.

*translation into American Sign Language—and when I asked him
what he thought it meant—he took his time and then responded in a
soft manner with his hands, "Loneliness."—and I just looked at
him and signed, "Yes!"*

In identifying with the life of a tree, Han was actually revisiting an image which pervades ancient mythology. If we accept reputed mythologist Joseph Campbell's definition of mythology as a collection of narratives which bear themes common to all mankind, Han's choice of the tree image is especially interesting. In myth, according to Campbell, the tree is often the metaphor for the rebirth of hope. This symbolism is reinforced in pagan, Christian and Egyptian mythology, as well as that of many African cultures.

"The sacred Tree, path to rebirth, symbol of the place of confluence of the human collective, draws the society together by directing its energy toward its powerful center."[*]

In choosing the image of a tree, Han could have been expressing his yearning for this powerful center, or a new family. If so, the hope couched in such a dream was to be realized. Lisa recalls the development of their three-year friendship leading to the evolution of Han's new life in America.

"Only after a period of ten weeks would a gradual thawing of fear begin to show itself. And it would take three years before Han would begin to feel secure in his new surroundings where a new family and community were to replace these elements of his Korean childhood. At the heart of his rehabilitation was the experience of performing theatre."[**]

*Halifax, *Shamanic Voices*, 15.
**Interview with author. February 3, 1998.

27

In a 1996 New York summer conference of the American Alliance for Theatre in Education, I attended a workshop conducted by Lisa where I was privileged to witness Han's videotaped performance of the haiku poem which he had chosen to dramatize. The vibrancy of his presentation with its irresistible musicality was remarkable, as eyes, fingers and body conjoined in a lively dance. It was as if Han, through Lisa's patient tutelage, had developed his personal voice.

In describing what Lisa Agogliati does, Sheila Doctors, former Supervisor of the Department of Special Education with whom Lisa Agogliati works, describes her appreciation for Lisa's achievements.

> *"Deaf students typically feel somewhat isolated in a hearing environment, reluctant to share their unique talents and abilities, for fear that their speech or language difficulties will limit their acceptance. What Ms. Agogliati has been able to do is to help students overcome these limits through movement, performance, and the magic of theatre."*[*]

Lisa sums up Han's evolution:

> *"I did not see him [Han] again until spring 1997, and he looked terrific. He seemed much more at ease with himself, and looking ahead with a positive attitude. He participated in my class once again, this time we focused on improvisation—and he contributed some great ideas—and had all of us laughing quite a bit with his 'comic' touch! Once he stayed after class to talk to me—and I thought he was going to ask to leave the course—but instead his question was to me 'How did I do? Did I do well with the drama?' It was a question I was so tickled to be asked—and I assured him*

---

*Brochure: Bethesda Academy of the Performing Arts: (6).

his work was fantastic and improving since we had worked to-gether a year ago."[*]

Epilogue: Three years later Lisa confirmed Han's notable progress.

The last time I saw him, I was wrapping up the residency and he was getting ready to graduate. He had been accepted into Gallaudet University, the nation's famous college for the deaf here in Washington, D.C., and I congratulated him on his accomplishment. It was then I saw, for what I hope would be many more to come, a beautiful smile on his face."[**]

Gueddy's Story
(DVD disc 2: section 5)

Rap, rap, rap . . . rap-a-rap-a rap-rap-rap. . . .

The heads of all in the rehearsal hall turned towards the court-yard door. But no one moved. Often a child would try to enter the recreation facility during evening rehearsals, and then, thinking better of it, would go on their way. Hoping this would be one of these instances, we continued rehearsing our young people's program which was to be offered in two weeks for the community of Santa Cruz, Bolivia.

But after a few more seconds . . .

RAP-RAP-RAP   . . .   BANG-BANG-BANG   . . . BOOM-BOOM-BOOM!!!

Whoever it was was *not* going away. A rehearsal assistant, Miranda Tarver, made her way swiftly to the locked door, urgently

---

*Agogliati, Lisa, telephone interview, August 3, 1997.
**Agogliati, Lisa, telephone interview, February 9, 2000.

shushed the little "pounder," and hustled him into a seat in the third row.

On that September evening in 2000, I was conducting mime classes with a small company of orphaned children at the Aldea SOS Children's Village in Santa Cruz, Bolivia. Four weeks previously I had received a phone call from a former college student and now a Peace Corps volunteer, Joseph W. Lown. JW informed me that the Director of the Aldea was looking for someone to teach theatre classes, and would I come. Four weeks later I was on the plane to Santa Cruz.

A mime program seemed to fit the need of the Bolivian orphans. Mime would eliminate language barriers, and I knew that children always enjoyed this theatre form. We were provided with a large recreation room for our rehearsals at the Aldea Infantiles SOS, a branch of a major institution dedicated to providing home and education for abandoned children worldwide. Six youngsters, from the ages ten to fourteen, were chosen, and we took up the work at eight each evening.

Our little intruder on this particular evening turned out to be a small boy passing by in the courtyard, who, seeing lights in the hall, was curious about what was going on inside. The locked door led to the volley of tattoos.

During a lull in the rehearsals, JW explained, "That's Gueddy. He's five years old—and deaf." The little gate-crasher with jet black hair and vibrant brown eyes seemed to realize that he was being discussed. He looked at me with a bright smile. (Plate 2)

This was the first time that Gueddy had ever witnessed theatre and he fell in love with it at first sight. He returned the next night, the next—and the next. By the fourth night, he had promoted himself and I found him perched beside me in the front row. He sat there blithely in a wooden chair, dressed in a faded blue shirt, shorts, and well-worn sneakers that dangled a full ten inches above the floor. His attitude seemed to say, *"Muy bien.* ("O.K.")

(Plate 2) Gueddy: the little gate-crasher seemed to realize that he was being discussed. He looked at me with a bright smile. (Photo courtesy of Miranda Tarver)

Let's see what goes on tonight." I felt I had acquired an assistant director.

One evening during our second week of rehearsals, the following scene took place. While I was giving rehearsal notes to two young actors who had just performed a comedy scene called "Los Pinteros" ("The Painters"), Nathaly, another member of the troupe, suddenly cried out excitedly, *"Mira! Mira lo que hace Gueddy!"* ("Look! Look what Gueddy is doing!")

We all turned to see. Gueddy was now standing center stage with a small paint can in one hand and a brush in the other. We could not believe our eyes. *After observing this complex eight minute number only once, this five-year-old child was repeating it to perfection!* When he finished, he could not hear our enthusiastic applause, of course, but the sight of laughing faces and wildly clapping hands left no doubt that he had delighted us. He stood before us beaming.

My curiosity was aroused. Could he possibly perform the number with a partner? I suspended the rehearsal, and we invited Diego, age fourteen, who played the role of the other painter, to act out the scene with Gueddy. Our astonishment grew. Gueddy demonstrated that he was completely adept at spontaneously "playing off" the actions of a partner. As any director knows, this is an intuitive talent extremely difficult to impart to one lacking a basic "feel" for comedy.

More surprises were to come.

Two nights later, also during a break, Gueddy once again took the stage. We sat transfixed as he developed the following scenario:

He began by carefully arranging ten of the recreation room's wooden chairs. He'd place a chair or two according to some inner logic which we were to discover. Then, stepping back to reflect, he'd shift their angles and positions ever so slightly. These meticulous arrangements and rearrangements took several minutes, until the composition was just right. What was going on in his little head? Then it became apparent. Ah! Gueddy was preparing for the visit of some friends.

Finally satisfied, Gueddy sat down quietly in contemplating his handiwork. But suddenly he leaped to his feet and disappeared behind a concrete archway. We waited for thirty seconds . . . a full minute. What was he *doing*?! No one dared break the spell. When he finally reappeared, he was "drying" his face with an imaginary towel. He'd been washing up for his special guests.

Soon he responded to a silent knock. Making a final alteration with two of the chairs, he opened an invisible door. Imaginary guests began to appear. Gueddy greeted each of them, indicating where they should sit. He then went from one to another in a series of individual encounters and we could fairly hear him asking, "How are you?" and "How have you been since I saw you last?" This accomplished, the gracious host sat in a contented stillness for over a full minute.

During the silence I was taken far outside of myself. For on this night, in a barren rehearsal hall on the remote plains of Santa Cruz de la Sierra, a timeless story was unfolding. It was as if the first actor was sharing his life with his community.

Gueddy's choice of a scenario seemed deeply significant. As in the story of Han, Gueddy, too, yearned for communion with his comrades. Owing to his hearing disability, he was denied this connection. He struggled valiantly to participate in his classes. He missed the jokes of his comrades. His confinement in his private world was accepted by all. But within this encapsulation the boy's genius had taken root. Now the theatre was providing this boy with a voice, and suddenly he was speaking volumes!

Our program plan called for four weeks of instruction. After several days, however, seeing the children having so much fun, JW and I decided to end my internship by offering a mime program for the community. The possibility was quickly picked up by the town cultural authorities. The forty-five-minute show would be presented on the final weekend on a Saturday afternoon at the

Casa de la Cultura—a large and stately nineteenth century building which served as the arts center for the community of Santa Cruz. The local press wrote about the coming event with great anticipation.

In view of Gueddy's remarkable talent, JW and I decided we must include him in the Casa de la Cultura program. There was only a week to go; we went right to work.

Live theatre is rare in Santa Cruz, and mime theatre even rarer. On the Saturday afternoon of the performance at the Casa de la Cultura, the long corridor space drew so many attendees that we had to offer two performances.

From the opening seconds of the show, an excited public seemed entranced by every move of our little troupe. An appreciative audience looked on with the greatest delight; moments of absolute silence were punctuated with bursts of explosive laughter. An elderly man in the second row laughed so heartily that he became a sideshow by himself!

As we finished our show, which did not include Gueddy's piece, there was extremely enthusiastic applause.

We did not wish to push Gueddy into a performance situation if it should make him uncomfortable in any way. But we should have known better; Gueddy needed no prodding! As the applause for the final number was subsiding, I saw him leaning forward excitedly in his seat in the wings, his entire body trembling with a wild desire to plunge onto the stage. His anxious expression said, "Now can I have my turn? . . . *Por favor*?"

A brief speech announcing the debut of our new actor was made. Enthusiastic applause. I reached under my chair for a little squeegee and extended it to Gueddy who grasped it proudly, and walked assuredly onto the stage to perform his acting debut in our newly created piece, "*El Lavador de Vidrios*" ("The Window Washer.")

The children of Santa Cruz are uniformly poor and usually in rags. You can see many of them at the street corners and at the traffic circles of the city holding little window squeegees and pails. They station themselves at the traffic lights in tense array. As the lights turn red, they swoop down on the delayed cars like a swarm of bees to honey. The idled motorists are helpless in this attack, and can only wave their hands wildly in attempts to drive them away. But the swarm will not be deterred. In a wild flurry, they fall to swabbing the windshields in the hopes of earning a half a boliviano, or about nine cents in American currency.

Our number proceeded as follows. Gueddy had stationed himself downstage in profile as an eager window washer. As a harried motorist on my way home, I sat in a chair, upstage center.

The action: As a rather grumpy driver is jolting along a pot-holed avenue in the chaos of rush hour, I begin a series of bumpy movements indicating the forward motion of the car. Gueddy, by contrast, initiates a sequence of smooth side-gliding steps toward me, creating the illusion that I am moving toward *him*. (He had mastered this tricky mime technique in rehearsals with no problem.)

Approaching a traffic light, I suddenly notice the boy before me. "*Caramba!*" I think, "I can't beat the light, and now I will be attacked by this mosquito in the bargain!" I brake the car and come abruptly to a halt. Gueddy's side-gliding movements come to a perfectly coordinated stop as my body lurches slightly forward.

A mimetic dialog follows:

"*Señor*, can I wash you? *Sí?*"

"No, no! go away!"

"*Por favor, señor. Por favor?!*"

"No! No! I say. *Vaya! Vaya!*" ("Go away!")

I object a third time even more strenuously. But by now the brazen mosquito is a delirious young seal, wildly flapping and slapping suds all over the windshield. I object further, but he loses no time in dousing the window on the passenger side as well. Finally, in an act of thoroughness that would shame many a professional *lavador* (window cleaner), he is energetically at work scrubbing *the rear window* as well!

The "swabber" is now suddenly at my side with an upturned palm. Reluctantly I fish into my pocket to comply. He quickly pockets the coin. But after a momentary reflection, he once more holds out his open hand. His look seems to say *"Por favor, señor,* couldn't you spare another for my 'seester?' " The audience howls and the man in the second row is holding his sides. "Highway robbery!" I fume. But fumbling and grumbling, I fish out another coin.

With an alacrity that elicits an audible gasp from the audience, the little *"lavador"* now reaches through the car window, adroitly removes my *eye-glasses* and washes *them as well*! as the audience explodes with paroxysms of laughter. The man in the second row is now so convulsed that the entire audience fears for his well-being.

With my hands on the steering wheel, the car lurches forward. As the receding body of the little *"lavador"* glides contentedly to the rear, I cannot suppress a tinge of affection. I look back. He waves a final *"Adios,"* which I wistfully reciprocate.

Deafening cheers proclaim a new star of the Bolivian stage! The next day Gueddy's picture is on the front page of *El Deber,* the town's leading journal. And soon after he is a front page item on other journals all over Bolivia. One article referred to him as *"el Pequeño Gigante"* ("the Little Giant"), as the renown of the famous *"lavador"* spread nationwide.

*   *   *

In April of 2001, I returned to Santa Cruz. The troupe, now officially named *Los Niños de Mi Corazón* (Children of My Heart) (Plate 3) was invited to perform alongside eighteen leading theatre companies from South America and Europe in The 3rd Annual International Theatre Festival held in Santa Cruz de la Sierra.

(Plate 3) The "Ninos de mi Corazón" Troupe that inspired thousands in South and North America. (Photo courtesy of Miranda Tarver)

Press, television and public were all now heralding the charms of the triumphant troupe from the orphanage. At the Festival dining room, in a touching gesture of homage, leading directors and actors from all parts of the globe would come to the table to congratulate our young actors.

Back home in the States, a year and a half later, after repeated petitions to the orphanage, permission was finally granted for a group of four of our *Niños* to perform in North America. After an official "no way" response from the government, the troupe was finally allowed to make the journey if accompanied by a chaperone, Andrea Lopez, the public relations director of the Aldea. The agreement was made, and Andrea turned out to be a lovely addition to our performing cast, filling in to cover for a young actor unable to make the trip.

My wife and I received all of the troupe in our home in southern Illinois for two weeks. During this time JW was constantly on the phone. "We have this fabulous performing group of orphan kids from Bolivia!" Many community audiences were eager to see the *Niños*, and soon we had a wide-ranging North American tour. A college alumnus generously loaned us a mini-bus. We also received unsolicited donations from all kinds of people who had heard of this story in newspapers and elsewhere, and wanted to cheer us on. At one school in West Virginia the children gave lunch money to the *Niños* so that they might enjoy a special meal!

We performed in Chicago, Virginia, and Washington, D.C.—where the children visited the Capitol, the Lincoln Memorial, and the Children's Museum at the Smithsonian. Our final stop was San Angelo, Texas. During the course of the tour, the *Niños* troupe touched the hearts of over 3600 who witnessed their performances.

By the time we reached San Angelo, Patch Adams, a famous M.D. who sponsors innumerable clown tours to all corners of the globe and was the subject of the movie, *Patch Adams,* heard of our story. A generous humanitarian, Adams immediately sent us an unsolicited donation to finance a hearing aid for Gueddy.

At the West Texas Rehabilitation Center of San Angelo, Gueddy was fitted for this hearing aid by Dr. Joel Jennings, one of America's leading audiologists. Gueddy's hearing is currently at 50%, permitting him to participate in his classes back in the Santa Cruz children's home for the first time. Recently, I received a happy letter from him with a sample of his striking artwork. He is now doing extremely well in his schoolwork, including his newly discovered talents at speech. In fact, he is speaking with the volubility of a dashing mountain stream, according to his former chaperone, Andrea, who adds that it is hard to stop him! He now plays games, jokes, and even imitates his teachers! In other words, he is finally doing those wonderful kid things for the first time.

It seems that everyone in our troupe has a success story of some kind or another. Andrea Cardona Lopez reported from Santa Cruz:

All the children of the troupe themselves have grown from the experience of theatre. Their studies have improved, and it has given them all an enormous boost of confidence. Two are now producing beautiful artwork. One of the actresses, Nathaly, now has her own website in La Paz with an identifying code, "la guapa ("good looking") .com."![*]

We also heard testimony of the positive effects of the performances on the attending children. An observation frequently heard from teachers was that these youngsters, most of whom were from minority and economically deprived groups, were given fresh hope. One superintendent commented, "All our kids were inspired by these abandoned children and came away with the feeling that now they could do the same."

Working with Bolivian orphans on three occasions, I became aware of how important a healthy atmosphere can be. These kids had no television, saw no movies and created their own amusements. And on three occasions, twice in Santa Cruz and then in a long North American tour, I saw no hint of pettiness, no hostility of any kind, and no evidence of complaint, even though they knew of how so many of the world's children had it better. There was only care, compassion and laughter.

How does this happen in our modern world? These teenagers had none of the gadgets of technology. A crumbled piece of paper served as a soccer ball, and two T-shirts, a pair of well-worn jeans

*Cardona, letter, April 14, 2004.

and a pair of crumbling sneakers, their wardrobe. I can recall the day when we were walking on the beggar-strewn sidewalks of Santa Cruz after their triumphant performance at the Santa Cruz Theatre Festival, JW Lown and I bought them all watches or a piece of jewelry. Nathaly, a lovely and spirited member of the troupe, preferred a pin that she saw in the window. She wore it to bed, I was told. One day my associate JW Lown, who had organized this program through the Peace Corps, and all of us stopped for an ice cream cone. It was like Christmas.

Commenting on the effects of Gueddy's success on the other children at the orphanage, JW Lown states:

All the kids at the orphanage and all who saw him in performances identified with him. He humanized their lives, filling them all with new hope. He showed them that they could achieve something in their own lives. His teachers who were once prone to relegate Gueddy to a neutral position in the classroom, now say, "We want to see him here" as one instructor put it recently. . . . The effect of Gueddy's success on his audiences, both in Bolivia and in North America, has been inspiring. Parents brought their children from all over Bolivia to see this boy, and to cheer him on. And through the theatre program the Aldea SOS itself has taken on a new pride.[*]

A happy footnote: JW Lown is currently celebrating his fifth anniversary as Mayor of San Angelo, the youngest mayor in the history of Texas. The entrepreneurial skill that JW developed in the *Niños* project was, according to him, a significant factor leading to his election. It is interesting how such an enterprise contains the potential to benefit all who participate in it.

*Honorable J. W. Lown, telephone interviews with author, April 29, 2004.

Many of the world's abandoned and disabled children are figuratively beating at the rehearsal doors of the world, yearning to be part of the action. We must see that these doors continue to swing open for them.

FOUR

A FOILED "SUICIDE," AND AN ENTIRE SCHOOL YEAR TURNED AROUND

It is a late January afternoon in 1978. The shabby basement assembly room of New York's P.S. 181, known as the Pablo Casals High School in the Bronx has become a theatre workshop. Some twenty young teenagers are convened for the third of four such weekly sessions sponsored by the New York State Council on the Arts. The fading afternoon sunlight which filters in through two large dust- clouded windows is supplemented by the glare of three overhead aluminum lamps. Rasa Allan, a veteran theatre teacher of the Richard Morse Mime Theatre, is in charge.

The class is largely composed of minority groups, including black, Hispanic, Chinese and Muslim children who have volunteered for a four-week series of after-school workshops. After three weeks of instruction in such mime techniques as the shaping of invisible tumblers, the opening of imaginary doors, and climbing non-existent staircases, the children are now integrating these techniques to tell their own stories. Sparked by the fun of transforming the familiar "*Snow White*" fairy tale into "*The Story of Snow Black,*" and "*The Three Musketeers*" into "*The Three Caballeros,*" the children are in the joyous throes of creation.

All except fourteen-year-old Geoffrey.

In the corner, a young boy of Hispanic origin with dark eyes

42

and hair and the unlikely name of Geoffrey has been sitting for three weeks in a shroud of defiant isolation. Hunched in his chair in the corner, with his sneakers drumming incessantly on the cement floor, he resembled a tightly coiled top about to break out into a wild spin.

According to his P.S. 181 teacher, Muriel Sokol, a pattern of surly hostility toward all authority characterized Geoffrey's behavior for the past year. The boy was raised by a single mother who never appeared at the school, and consequently, neither Mrs. Sokol nor the school principal knew much about him or his background. He seemed to be one of many Co-Op City children with little to do in after school hours but roam the streets.

According to Mrs. Sokol, death had been often on Geoffrey's mind. He had failed in two suicide attempts through overdosing on aspirin. He was currently coasting through the eighth grade with a poor academic record. There was scant hope that he would graduate to the ninth.

Why had Geoffrey stuck with this voluntary after-school theatre workshop? After all, he wasn't required to be here. An observation from authority on classroom drama, David Booth, seemed to explain the scene. In his book, *Story Drama*, the author observes:

> *Some children simply tag along until suddenly the situation, the tension of the group pulls them inside the drama.*[*]

Notwithstanding Geoffrey's aloofness during the first two weeks, it seemed apparent to Ms. Allan that in this third session something was stirring.

With the penultimate Friday class drawing to a close, volunteers were invited to present their stories at the final meeting the

---

*Booth, *Story Drama*, 89.

next week. Suddenly, Geoffrey's hand shot upward. In a frantic effort to inscribe his name in her small yellow pad before he might change his mind—instructor Allan all but broke her pencil lead!

At the final Friday afternoon session, after two brief skits, it was Geoffrey's turn. Ms. Allan took a deep breath and nonchalantly called his name. Yes, he meant business all right. He picked up a solid six-foot wooden board that he had found lying near the schoolyard dumpster and placed it over the seats of two wooden chairs. Identifying this structure as the tenth-floor high-rise apartment occupied by his family, he then convened a pre-chosen supporting cast of six friends. The group entered into a secret caucus to absorb some final stage directions.

The following scene took place and was recorded on a crude hand-held videotape recorder.

Action! Geoffrey enters slowly from audience right, stops and furtively glances from one side to another. The coast is clear. Utilizing a mime technique that he observed in the class, he begins to climb an invisible staircase. The ten flights are managed with dispatch. (Malfunctioning elevators were commonplace to the residents of the project.) Arriving "breathless" at the tenth floor, Geoffrey unlocks and enters the imaginary front door to his apartment. Next, he crosses to an invisible window just to the left of the plank, which he opens carefully. Stepping through the window onto the "window ledge," he makes his way gingerly to the center. Here he hesitates and teeters precariously "ten stories" above the sidewalk.

Enter the supporting cast: Geoffrey's six classmates saunter casually onto the sidewalk ten stories below. All at once, the chorus leader stops and shielding his eyes, glances upward.

"Hey look! Up dayuh!" he exclaims. All now peer upward squinting and shading their eyes.

"Who's dat?" one cries out.

"Hey, thass' Geoffrey!"

A chorus of disbelief: "Naw! Naw!"

Anti-chorus: "Sí! Sí, Thass' Geoffrey!"

"No!" "Sí!" "Naw, man!" "Sí!"

"*Mira, mira*! Thass' Geoffrey all right!"

The chorus leader cups his hands over his mouth: "GEOFFREY, WHACHU DOIN'?"

From ten stories up: "I'M GONNA JUMP, MAN. LOOK OUT!"

"Naw, don' do dat, man!"

"Yeah, man, get outta' da' way!"

"No, man! Wait man, wait!"

A quick and desperate huddle below. Then, "Wait a secun', man, we got somethin' t' tell ya'."

"No, man, go 'way!"

"Wait, jes' wait!"

The rescue unit breaks, establishing two imaginary stairways, one left and one right. Two rescuers mount the stairs while four lend moral support from below. Arriving breathlessly at the tenth floor, the two heroic rescuers creep out onto the ledge from opposite sides. Flailing attempts to grasp Geoffrey's elusive hands produce a demonstration of high-level teetering that would do credit to any Barnum and Bailey high-wire act. Finally, one of the rescuers succeeds in grasping Geoffrey's left hand, and the right is avidly clamped by the other. The three lurch precariously on the plank, as the team below attempts to instill confidence. "Take it easy, man!" "Thass it!" "Thass it!" and finally, "Hurray!" as Geoffrey is seized and ushered back through the left window. Geoffrey and his four rescuers clatter helter-skelter down to the street where they are all greeted by their relieved friends. "Yea!" "Hurray!!" "Man that was close!" "Just in time, man!" and "Man, you betta not do dat again!"

What followed was a group embrace of such intensity that the rescued Geoffrey was completely lost from sight for thirty seconds. The video camera entered into the act, bumping around the room, revealing blank walls, an exit door and a screaming audience. When the lens finally located Geoffrey, one feared for his life! He was now a human trampoline with the group pummeling and bouncing on him mercilessly. Finally, lifting the distraught Geoffrey onto their shoulders the wildly cheering rescuers carried him off in triumph.

Mrs. Sokol later reported that this moment represented a turning point in Geoffrey's school life. Through the dramatization of a life problem, he had bonded with his class. And to her knowledge, he never talked of death again.

Here is an unsolicited letter which she wrote in gratitude for what the theatre experience had meant to her class, and especially to Geoffrey.

PABLO CASALS
P.S. 181 BRONX
Feb. 14, 1978

Dear Rasa,

Brava! Brava! Brava! You have been unanimously chosen "Mime of the Year" by all classes meeting in Room 161 and particularly by their teacher.

You helped turn a year that promised to be a disaster into a howling success—the highlight of my teaching career.

Oh the joy you have brought into teaching and the effect of mime and movement on my pupils!

To be more specific, let me tell you what I have observed.

First of all there is a new self-awareness, an ability to feel more deeply and to channel and control emotions. Communication skills have improved and there's a new understanding of group cooperation.

Secondly, by creating and "trying on" characters, an insight into others has developed. As well as a sensitivity to their feelings. Thirdly, and most important, by freeing their bodies and minds and guiding the children to focus on the activity of the moment, the door to intellectual development has been flung wide open for them.

Although I have no "soap box" to orate from, I have been addressing other school faculty conferences as well as my own trying to share with them how beautifully effective were your visits to my classroom—the life you injected into Geoffrey who up to that point only dwelled on death; the guidance counselor's joy at seeing so many of her pupils successfully and cooperatively perform for the school.

Rasa, you reached them all. The intellectually gifted, the slow learner and the "in between." You illuminated each of their lives with a new sense of self-worth.

I wish that every teacher could have the opportunity to work with you and Richard and your wonderful Mime Theatre. However, as for me, I am eternally grateful and so glad you were mime. (sic!)

Affectionately,
Muriel Sokol

I feel that in all probability Mrs. Sokol had no formal knowledge of Theatre-in-Education theory. And yet what she had touched upon here virtually defines theatre's potential as a rehabilitative force. Consider the themes Mrs. Sokol identifies in this remarkable letter.

"a new self-awareness"
"an ability to feel more deeply and to channel and control emotions"

"communication skills [have] improved"
"a new understanding of group cooperation"
"an insight into others and a sensitivity to their feelings"

Then, on the academic side:

"By freeing their bodies and minds and guiding the children to focus on the activity of the moment, the door to intellectual development has been flung wide open."

These remarks of Mrs. Sokol identify two principal areas where theatre in the classroom is so effective: (1) the potential to bring emotional stability and bonding to our young people; and (2) as a strong contributory influence to academic studies.

Part II

Pioneers and Their Followers

FIVE

ROOTS OF THE THEATRE-IN-EDUCATION MOVEMENT: FREEING THE CHILD TO LEARN

Before the Theatre-in-Education (TIE) movement could occur, key classroom reforms in the European and American educational system were needed. These arrived in the eighteenth century through the pioneering work of Jean Jacques Rousseau, Johann Pestalozzi and Frederich Froebel, and were integrated two centuries later into the educational theory of the American philosopher, John Dewey. What we refer to as the Theatre-in-Education movement today is rooted in these reforms.

Jean Jacques Rousseau (1712–1778)

Self-actualizing of the student

Jean Jacques Rousseau was born in Geneva and enjoyed a happy childhood which was characterized by a close contact with nature. He moved to Paris, but found the corrupting influences of city life inimical to the child's early development. In 1762 Rousseau published his two major writings, *Du Contrat Social (The Social Contract)*, and *Émile: ou l'Éducation (Émile, on Education)*.

51

L'Éducation consists of a detailed series of recommendations for the educational development of a fictional pupil, Émile.

The European classroom was not a happy place when Rousseau arrived in the French capital. Instruction was a one-way system in which the professor's word was law. In an examination, the pupil was expected to repeat just what the professor had expounded in his lecture, and of course this process allowed no space for investigation, deduction or reflection of any kind on the part of the pupil. Roussseau found this "one way" system intolerable. He wrote in his *Émile:*

> *"Je ne connais rien de plus inepte que çe mot 'Je vous l'avais bien dit,"* or, roughly translated, *"I know of nothing more pointless than the phrase, 'It is so because I have said it."*[*]

If the instructor judged the student's responses inadequate, he used the humiliating convention of the "dunce cap," where the student was made to sit in an isolated corner of the classroom wearing a high, conical hat. Cruel physical punishment was also meted out through the practice of caning, where the student would be tied to a post and whipped with a birch rod. Each of these "corrective" measures was widely practiced across Europe.

What Rousseau sought was to reform these cruel and humiliating methods. In *Émile* he proposed a collaborative teacher-pupil relationship, but behind this, there was a need to respect the child and childhood.

> *Hommes, soyez humains, c'est votre premier devoir: soyez-le pour tous les états, pour tous les âges, pour tout ce qui n'est étranger à l'homme. Quelle sagesse y a-t-il pour vous hors de l'humanité? Aimez l'enfance: favorisez ses jeux, ses plaisirs, son aimable instinct. Qui de vous n'a pas regretté quelquefois cet âge où le rire est*

---

[*]Rousseau: 1911. Garniers Frères. (285)

toujous sur les lèvres, et ou l'âme est toujours en paix? Pourquoi voulez-vous ôter à ces petits innocents la jouissance d'un temps si court qui leur échappe, et d'un bien si précieux dont ils ne sauraient abuser? Pourquoi voulez-vous remplir d'amertume et de douleurs ces premiers ans si rapides, qui ne reviendront pas plus pour eux qu'ils ne peuvent revenir pour vous?

Men, be humane, this is your first duty; be thus for all times, for all ages, for all that which befits mankind. What wisdom is there beyond humanity? Love childhood; encourage its games, its pleasures, its lovable instincts. Which of you has not missed at one time or another, that age when laughter was always on the lips and the soul always at peace? Why would you wish to deprive these innocents of the joy of a time so short and fleeting, and of a pleasure so precious they wouldn't know how to abuse? Why would you wish to fill these first years, which are so fleeting and which will never return to them any more than to you, with bitterness and sadness?[*]

To remedy this harsh alienation between professor and pupil, Rousseau proposed that the student be free to make his own deductions, and thus take responsibility for his own learning process. The student would first be encouraged to form deductions from nature studies, and then there would be a collaboration between instructor and child. Of course this represented a threat to authority and to faculty which they, as bearers of age-old traditions, would never relinquish.

Protests were raised: "How can the student be trusted to learn through his own efforts?!" Rousseau replied:

Give them full use of such strength as they have; they will not misuse it.[**]

*Rousseau, Jean Jacques. *Émile.* Garnier Frères. Book II (57)
**Rousseau. 1911. (35)

"But am I to understand that a student will be interested enough to learn on his own?" the voices continued. "Indeed! My students are interested in nothing, least of all learning. I have to drum it into them!''

Rousseau replied that students must be led to perceive how it was to their advantage to learn. In other words, before the child can read, send him an invitation to something he loves. He'll learn to read that in a hurry! Rousseau was himself anticipating theatre-in-education philosophy.

If I wanted to teach rhetoric to a youth whose passions were as yet undeveloped, I would draw his attention continually to things that would stir his passions, and I would discuss with him how he should talk to people so as to get them to regard his wishes favorably.[*]

Passion? No one had mentioned "passion" in connection with education before! Copies of *Émile* fueled bonfires in the Sorbonne courtyard and then in the public squares of Geneva. For Rousseau, passion, enthusiasm and joy were causes of rejection, showing how society treated Émile.

The academic community was further enraged by the concepts of *pleasure* and *play* that would accompany the learning process. Suggesting that play enter the classroom must have seemed like asking the faculties of Europe to exchange their austere black robes for clown motley. Nevertheless, the concept of play courses as a prancing pony throughout *Émile*.

Work and play are all the same to him (Émile). His games are his occupations; he is not aware of any difference. He goes into everything he does with a pleasing interest and freedom. It is indeed a

*Rousseau, Ib. (214)

charming spectacle to see a nice boy of this age with open smiling countenance, doing the most serious things in his play, profoundly occupied with the most frivolous amusements.[*]

The training of the senses in Émile was essential to all future growth. Carefully cultivated sensory training would facilitate sound intellectual and moral judgments that would be required of him in later years.

Consider his senses, his inventive mind, his foresight. Consider the good head he will have. He will want to know all about everything he sees and does, and will take nothing for granted. He will refuse to learn anything until he acquires the knowledge that is implied in it. When he sees a spring made he will want to know how the steel was got from the mine. If he sees the pieces of a box put together, he will want to know how the tree was cut. When he is using a tool himself he will not fail to say of the tool he uses: "If I did not have this tool, how would I make one like it, or manage without it?" . . .
The senses are the first faculties to take form and mature in us. They should therefore be the first to be cultivated. They are generally the ones most neglected. To train them calls for more than the use of them. It means learning to judge properly by them: learning, one might say, to feel. We do not know how to touch, see or hear until we have learned.[**]

The training of the senses would also serve to develop judgment, enabling Émile to make sound decisions in every area of his later life and establish him as an independent thinker.

Give him the facts and let him judge for himself. That is how he will learn to know men. If he is always guided by some author's judg-

[*]William Boyd, Ed. *The Émile of Jean Jacques Rousseau.* 1956. (67)
[**]Ibid. (87)

ment, he only sees through another's eyes: when he lacks these eyes he cannot see. [*]

It is significant that the only book to be allowed Émile was *Robinson Crusoe.* In the Defoe novel, the protagonist is shipwrecked on a desert island, and called upon to survive through the use of his instincts. Through the use of this intuition which has been developed through a training of the senses, Robinson Crusoe survives his ordeal, and so will Émile if he follows Crusoe's example. The metaphor is plain: the society waiting to confront Émile is *itself* a jungle.

This instinctive approach to experience led to the term "noble savage" derided by Rousseau's critics. But the concept of the savage was not to be demeaned, but exalted, according to Rousseau. The "savage," in Rousseau's lexicon, represents the natural instincts upon which our earthly survival depends.

Émile is not a savage to be banished to the deserts: he is a savage made to live in a town. [**]

Rousseau's curriculum sets out what must be introduced to achieve this at each stage of Émile's growth. The gradation of the learning process prescribed by Rousseau was as follows: From the ages of 3 to 6 years, the education of Émile would consist of nature studies in which he would make his own deductions, developing the child's powers of observation. From the ages of 6–12, games and play would be encouraged to acquire the improvisational skills necessary for survival, in much the same way that animals learn survival skills through play. From 12 to 15 the child, now a young adult, would learn practical matters, such as the exploration

*Ibid. (108)
**Ibid. (92)

of a profession. Finally, from 15 to 20, and not until then, the pupil would be permitted to reflect on philosophy, morality and the means of creating a harmonious society.[*]

This tiered method of learning was not a restriction, but a protection to Émile. Worldly and burdensome theories of psychology and philosophy would be proscribed, until the child had developed the mental readiness to absorb these.[**]

Contemporary educator, Neil Postman, in his *The Disappearance of Childhood,* emphasizes, as Rousseau did two centuries ago, what is at stake in exposing our children to a premature surfeit of worldly knowledge:

> *The world of the known and the not yet known is bridged by wonderment. But wonderment happens largely in a situation where the child's world is separate from the adult world. As media merge the two worlds, as the tension created by secrets to be unraveled is diminished, the calculus of wonderment changes. Curiosity is replaced by cynicism, or even worse, arrogance. We are left with children who rely not on authoritative adults but on news from nowhere. We are left with children who are given answers to questions they never asked. We are left, in short, without children.[***]*

With respect to the content of the curriculum, Rousseau proposed that dry classical studies which bore no relationship with the student's own experience would be replaced by those which sought to empower the student to function in his immediate environment.

> *To live in the world he must know how to get on with other people, he must know what forces move them, he must calculate the action*

[*]Rousseau, Jean Jacques. Nouvelle Edition. Paris, Librairie Garnier Frères. (1911) Livre 1 (Book 1)
[**]Rousseau, Jean Jacques, 1911. (21)
[***]Postman, Neil. *Disappearance*, 1982. (90)

*and reaction of self-interest in civil society, he must estimate the
results so accurately that he will rarely fail in his undertakings, or
he will at least have tried in the best possible way.**

The curriculum of Rousseau is thus designed to respond to
stages of growth: infancy, childhood, the approach of adolescence, adolescence, the age of humanity (Émile at 18), and the
coming of manhood. There is even an add-on section on marriage.
By this stage Émile's talents for discernment in social matters will
extend to his choice of an ideal mate. But let us not lift a premature
eyebrow. No need for Internet dating services here! If Émile has
acquired good taste in all other spheres, he and his ideal partner,
Sophie, will enjoy a long and ideal conjugality. And why not? If
Rousseau's theories can resolve so many of the world's problems,
why not apply them, similarly, to the arrangement that has produced so much of the world's angst?**

Rousseau's theories included no specific proposals for a new
curriculum in *Émile*, which was rather intended as a plea for a humane classroom atmosphere.

*This collection of scattered thoughts and observations has little
order or continuity; it was begun to give pleasure to a good mother
who thinks for herself. . . Fathers and mothers, do things your own
way. May I count on your good will?****

To read *Émile*, if one is susceptible to a kind of academic ro-

---

*Rousseau, Jean Jacques. 1956. (212–213)

**The only skeptical note in *Émile* seems to be the contemplation of what would follow the
happy marriage of Émile and Sophie. Love invariably turns into less felicitous times, according to Rousseau, and the only remedy—which contemporary marriage counselors
have hardly improved upon—lies in the renewal of romance—not necessarily with
Sophie!

***Ib. Preface.

manticism, is to be stirred by a declaration of the highest originality. The English essayist, Charles Lamb, wrote that seeing Kean act Shakespeare was like reading Shakespeare to flashes of lightning. Reading Rousseau can be a bit like that. Whatever its excesses and generalities, whatever its faults, it beckons us to exhilarating heights in urging openness, generosity and kindness in teaching our young.

The call to arms for a progressive education had been sounded which was to be echoed to our times in the practice of many pioneer educators. These included such disciples as John Dewey, Maria Montessori, and Rudolf Steiner. By progressive education, we refer to an educational approach which seeks to develop not only the intellectual and scholarly capacities of the child, but those of his moral, spiritual and social values as well.[*]

The proposed reforms of Rousseau that were to influence education to our day and open the gateway for the liberating methods of the theatre-in-education movement, may be summarized as follows:

- Replacing the infallible authority of the professor with a stimulation of curiosity which would lead the student to question.

- Establishing a collaborative relationship between student and professor.

- Utilizing sensory perception, play, and experimentation in acquiring knowledge.

*More can be learned about holistic education today through the writings of Ron Miller, the founder of *The Holistic Education Review.* A wealth of additional information on "holistic education" may also be found through contacting the website *www.infed.org/biblio/holisticeducation.htm*

- Devising a curriculum that encourages the child's spiritual and moral development, as well as the intellectual, by permitting him to occupy a productive and harmonious place in his surrounding world.

Perhaps there is no educator to this day who has inspired such controversy as Rousseau. Educator Lawrence A. Cremin writes:

In the two hundred years since its publication in 1762, Rousseau's Émile *has been the subject of endless controversy. The work was ordered burned in Paris and Geneva within weeks of its appearance; yet it was read passionately throughout Europe. Goethe called it "the teacher's gospel," while Kant maintained that no book had ever moved him so deeply. Its influence has been prodigious; and even such an unrelenting critic as William T. Harris who once referred to Rousseau's teaching as "the greatest heresy in educational doctrine," felt impelled to remark that apart from the Émile there could be no understanding Pestalozzi, Froebel, Basedow, or for that matter any other educator of the nineteenth century. Within this context it is well, perhaps, to note a judgment Professor Boyd himself rendered a half-century ago at the beginning of a long and distinguished career in the field of education. "I believe," he wrote in* The Educational Theory of Jean Jacques Rousseau *"that the Émile with all its faults is the most profound modern discussion of the fundamentals of education, the only modern work of the kind worthy to be put alongside the Republic of Plato. . . . I am only a disciple in the sense that I have learned and continue to learn a great deal from him. Whether agreeing or disagreeing, I have found no other thinker on educational questions so stimulating or so enlightening. Under his guidance it seems to me one gets to the very heart of the great problems of democratic education which are still perplexing us." For my part, I know of no better definition of a classic.*[*]

---

*Cremin, Lawrence A., *The Emile of Jean Jacques Rousseau.* Preface. (1956)

Johann Heinrich Pestalozzi (1745–1827)

The classroom as family

The first major educator to activate the principles of Rousseau was the Swiss pedagogue, Johann Heinrich Pestalozzi. This devoted disciple honored his mentor by naming his son Jean Jacques, and also called for an education which would be rooted in extensive contacts with nature. Pestalozzi's great contribution to education, however, was his conception of the classroom as a working family.

Pestalozzi was a deeply caring and heroic figure who, in his first days as a teacher, sheltered many abandoned children from the 1798 French invasion of Switzerland. He would encounter much opposition from officialdom in pedagogical circles. His second source of anguish was the continual poverty that followed him throughout his life. Biographer Kate Silber records these extremely difficult times.

The family in the Neuhof was now utterly destitute and often lacked the barest essentials. Pestalozzi later told the story of how, when other people were sitting down to a meal, he would wander about in the fields, eating a piece of dry bread and drinking water from the brook with it. He did not dare to go either to town or to church because he had no decent clothes. He became "the laughing stock of the people"; the mob called him "Pestilence" or "Scarecrow," jeering "Wherever he goes, the birds fly away." With the loss of his money he had also forfeited public confidence in himself and in his true capacity. His Zurich friends avoided him; when they espied him at the top of a street they would go down another, for to have been obliged to speak to a man so far beyond help would only have embarrassed them and been of no use to him. Pestalozzi relates in his Swansong how Caspar Fusli, the bookseller "told me at that time to my face, my old friends took it for granted that I would end my days in an almshouse or even in a madhouse." In-

*deed, Pestalozzi lived through a period of deep depression; with despairing heart and mind confused he roamed through fields and woods; even his wife had almost given him up; to himself his life seemed "only nonsense and raving madness."**

Pestalozzi somehow found a way to survive these harsh conditions in seeing his schools at Burgdorf and Yverdon, Switzerland, established as model institutions of learning for visiting teachers from all over Europe and America.

Pestalozzi's first labors were bent toward the elevation of dispossessed segments of society. He began by taking in fifty beggar children in 1774, at his farm in Neuhof, Switzerland, where he instructed them in a home-school environment. Pestalozzi taught these abandoned children reading, writing, and mathematics, and, in addition, introduced them to the practical techniques of gardening, farming and cheese-making. After two years, with funds depleted, the experiment came to a forced end, but this impasse served only to spur the Swiss educator to greater efforts in creating an educational method which would benefit all levels of society.

Highly influenced by Rousseau, who was to become his mentor and spiritual guide, Pestalozzi also encouraged his children to learn from what he termed "*sense impression,*" or through direct observation of nature. During the first eight years of schooling, the child would be free to gather its own impressions from nature under the mother's guidance, as detailed in his *A Book for Mothers.* This acquisition of natural law would strengthen the child's deductive powers and lead to the articulation of language.

In a later period during the operation of his school at Yverdon, Pestalozzi would address his children and faculty on deeply spiritual and moral issues:

*Silber, Kate, *Pestalozzi.* 1973. (26)

The weekly address on Saturday evenings was always given by Pestalozzi himself. He then surveyed what had been done during the week, using the everyday happenings as starting-points for comments on the broader issues of life. Or he dealt with religious principles, relating them to the children's own experiences. He spoke on the futility of knowledge without love but also on the uselessness of love without knowledge. His aim was to evoke a religious spirit in the children and to make the desire for a good life "habitual" in them. [*]

In the pedagogical methods of Pestalozzi, we note the first example of a close collaboration—which Rousseau had advocated—between student and teacher. In this case the intellectual and spiritual partnership took the form of a working family. On an official investigation of Pestalozzi's farm school at Yverdon, an inspector remarked: "This is quite an astonishing fact that I find the atmosphere of the school one of a great family." [**]

Author Kate Silber records:

The Yverdon children looked intelligent because their education was "natural," and they were happy because there was friendship and confidence between masters and pupils. During the first and best years of its existences true family spirit pervaded the House, and more than by any public recommendation was Pestalozzi satisfied by a word from a simple peasant: "This is not an institute, it is a household." [***]

A public statue at Yverdon, honoring the life and spirit of this great educator, catches the inspired quality of the man. In this statue, Pestalozzi is striding gently but resolutely forward with

*Silber, Kate. 1973. (211)
**Cubberly, Ellwood P., *History*. 1920. (192)
***Silber, Kate. 1973. (211)

two children on either side grasping affectionately at his coattails.[*]
Other lithographs depicting the atmosphere of the Pestalozzi
schoolroom attest to the family atmosphere. Children are grouped
haphazardly around the floor engaged in playful wrestling, or
reading books, with others working at a low table. The lithographs
give the impression of a harmonious and bonded clan.

Pestalozzi's devotion to the child and to the poor was rooted
in deeply religious convictions, which were also reflected strongly
in the writing and theory of Frederich Froebel. Both expressed
their convictions that education was rooted in a love of God, a God
Who directed His followers first and foremost to care for the poor
and needy.

As Pestalozzi revered Rousseau, so Frederich Froebel was
deeply influenced by Pestalozzi.

Frederich Froebel (1782–1852)

Pioneer of the Kindergarten

*What exuberant life! What immeasurable enjoyment! What un-
bounded activity! What an evolution of physical forms! What a
harmony between the inner and outer life!*
—Excerpt from Lange's *Reminiscences of Froebel.*

Born in 1782, Froebel was possessed of a gentle nature which
was much misunderstood by his father. Biographer W.N.

---

[*]In the spring of 1997 The Richard Morse Mime Theatre gave a series of special performances at the Don Guanella School in Milan, Italy. Guanella was a beloved priest who had
also formed a school for orphaned children. At the entrance of the school was a statue com-
memorating the humane works of this revered educational leader, don Guanella, flanked
by two children in an affectionate attitude virtually replicating this statue of Pestalozzi. It
was a moving moment for us all.

Hailmann describes this strained relationship and the influences that would later reveal themselves as central to Froebel's career as an important world educator.

His father, who was the laborious pastor of several parishes, seems to have been solely occupied with his duties and to have given no concern whatever to the development of the child's mind and character beyond that of strictly confining him within doors, lest he should come to harm by straying away. One of his (young Froebel's) principal amusements, he tells us, consisted in watching from the window some workmen who were repairing the church, and he remembered long afterward how he earnestly desired to lend a helping hand himself. The instinct of construction, for the exercise of which, in his system, he makes ample provision was even then stirring within him. As years went on, though nothing was done for his education by others, he found opportunities for satisfying some of the longings of his soul, by wandering in the woods, gathering flowers, listening to the birds, or to the wind as it swayed the forest trees, watching the movements of all kinds of animals, and laying up in his mind the various impressions then produced, as a store for future years. [*]

Here we note the early impulses in Froebel's childhood, the absorption with nature and the fascination with geometric shapes, which were to inspire his educational system called "the play way." In this method, Froebel would utilize building blocks of all shapes and sizes to stimulate the imagination of the child in developing his Kindergarten—or "child garden" system.

During the summer of 1805, while he was studying architecture and teaching in Frankfort-on-Main, Froebel visited Pestalozzi for two weeks in Yverdon. He was overwhelmed by what he observed. After a return visit in 1808, his career fell into focus, as he

*Hailmann, W. N. New York. 1887. (11)

moved quickly toward a life work of teaching and his role as originator of the Kindergarten system, a method of teaching now in worldwide use.

It was Froebel's belief that the early years of schooling were the most crucial to a child's development. In Froebel's theory, the instinct for creating harmonious forms in childhood would help to establish harmonious relationships throughout a lifetime. Froebel also insisted that this early training would translate into a moral and spiritual development contributing to a firm relationship with God.

> *Education should lead and guide man to clearness concerning himself, to peace with nature, and to unity with God; hence, it should lift to a knowledge of himself and of mankind to a knowledge of God and of nature, and to the pure and holy life in which such knowledge leads.* [*]

As Pestalzozzi before him, Froebel conceived of teaching as a deeply religious activity:

> *Genuine and true, living religion, reliable in danger and in struggles, in times of oppression and need, in joy and pleasure, must come to man in his infancy; for the Divine Spirit that lives and is manifest in the finite in man, has an early though dim feeling of its divine origin; and the vague sentiment, this exceedingly misty feeling, should be fostered, strengthened, nurtured and later, raised into full consciousness, into clear apprehension.* [**]

Play, so long denied the child in the halls of learning, was now becoming a cause célèbre. Today virtually all of our prominent educational theorists and progressive educators acknowledge

[*]Froebel, *Education*, 2, 3.
[**]Froebel, *The Education of Man*, 25.

that when play accompanies lessons, the child learns better. Twentieth century educator Richard Courtney writes:

What consequence does play have on our lives? . . . The player's actions are the nub of existence. C.S. Pierce says we conceive of possibility in play; its meaning lies with what the player does. Play for William James provides us with knowledge—not within it, but as a result of it. . . . Play is a social concept, mind and self are social emergents, and inquiry is its essence. The child knows Christopher Columbus or numbers by re-playing them. Reality is what we know when we play. [*]

Froebel states that the positive influences of play encouraged in childhood, would take root to produce harmonious overtones for a lifetime:

Play is self-active representation of the inner—a representation of the inner from inner necessity and impulse. The plays of childhood are the germinal leaves of all later life; for the whole man is developed and shown in these, in his tenderest dispositions, in his innermost tendencies. The whole later life of man, even to the moment, when he shall leave it again, has its source in this period of childhood. [**] *. . .* <u>God creates and works productively in uninterrupted continuity.</u> *Each thought of God is a work, a deed, a product; and each thought of God continues to work with creative power in endless productive activity to all eternity.* [***] *(Emphasis of Froebel)*

---

*Courtney, *Play, Drama and Thought*, 52.
**Froebel, *Education*, 322.
***Froebel, *Memoir*, 30.

John Dewey (1859–1952)

The entire world as a laboratory

John Dewey is generally regarded as the pre-eminent American philosopher of the 20th Century. His philosophic inquiry spans the fields of logic, science, esthetics, art, education, interpretation of history and personal and individual social psychology. His insistence on the need for direct experience in verifying knowledge has often led to the term "social pragmatist" in describing Dewey. His influence on education has extended from Western society to find adherents in China and Japan, largely from his Oriental lecture tours in the 1930's.

Dewey's educational theories form a natural bridge, as we shall note, from the thinking of Rousseau, Pestalozzi and Froebel, to the foundations of Theatre-in-Education movement in the early twentieth century.

As with Rousseau two centuries before, Dewey passed a happy childhood characterized by a close contact with nature. During these youthful days in Vermont, he made frequent canoe trips, and these contributed to a curiosity about the natural world.

Dewey's own education placed a strong emphasis on classical studies, including Greek, Latin, the sciences, history, and philosophy. The philosophers Kant, Locke, Hume, Hegel, and William James were influential in Dewey's development, and the writings of James in particular, articulating pragmatic theory, contributed substantially to Dewey's educational philosophy.

John Dewey's studies took him from the University of Vermont, to teaching posts at the Massachusetts Institute of Technology, Johns Hopkins, Columbia and The University of Michigan.

Dewey was one of the pioneers of what is called "progressive education," which strove to equip the student to function harmoniously in a changing world. To appreciate his contribution to education, and to the Theatre-in-Education movement in particular, we must first examine what the learning experience was like in the 1890's, or the period when Dewey began his reforms, which reveals little change since the days of Rousseau (or the Middle Ages!). Oscar Handlin observes in his *John Dewey's Challenge to Education:*

> *The realm of the classroom in the 1890's was totally set off from the experience of the child who inhabited it. The teachers' lessons encrusted by habit, the seats arranged in formal rows, and the rigid etiquette of behavior all emphasized the difference between school and life. Hence learning consisted of a tedious memorization of data without a meaning immediately clear to the pupil. . . . Dewey, whose own education as a boy was free of all such rigidity, objected strenuously that these conditions stifled the learning process, for they prevented the student from relating his formal studies to his own development as a whole person.*[*]

Dewey's mission was to narrow the gap between the classroom and the world that surrounded it. This would begin with the child's immersion in nature studies, as Rousseau had prescribed almost two centuries before.

> *Again, we cannot overlook the importance for educational purposes of the close and intimate acquaintance got with nature at first hand, with real things and materials, with the actual processes of their manipulation, and the knowledge of their social necessities and uses. In all this there was continual training of observation, of ingenuity, constructive imagination, of logical thought, and of the sense of reality acquired through first hand contact with actualities.*[**]

Rousseau insisted that this absorption with nature would

*Handlin, *Challenge*, 52.
**Dewey, *The Child*, 11.

69

serve to lead the student toward an understanding of life experience in ways that a concentration on facts, theories and memorization could never provide. Dewey amplified this thought:

> *The point that I have been wishing so far to make is that the possibility of having knowledge become something more than the mere accumulation of facts and laws, of becoming actually operative in character and conduct, is dependent on the extent to which that information is evolved out of some need in the child's own experience and to which it receives application to that experience.*[*]

This new approach to pedagogy, through its replacement of passive reading or listening by actual doing, would produce a renewed pleasure in learning, predicted Dewey. And subject matter itself was thrown wide open for the first time.

> *A clique, a club, a gang, a Fagin's household of thieves, the prisoners in a jail, provide educative environments for those who enter into their collective or conjoint activities, as truly as a church, a labor union, a business partnership, or a political party. Each of them is a mode of associated or community life, quite as much as is a family, a town, or a state.*[**]

Educator Lawrence A. Cremin details the many changes that have evolved in American society since the 17th Century days of home schooling in America which have dictated emphasis on practical learning. These social conditions included the need to operate

> *. . . the factory, but also the mine, the shop, the office, the retail establishment, and the government bureau; custodial institutions with the explicit purpose of rehabilitating their clients; . . . the*

*Dewey, *Lectures*, 80, 81.
**Dewey, *Democracy in Education*, 21.

other factors urged by the exigencies of a more dispersed and industrialized society. [*]

Dewey observed these changes and recognized that an education of a practical nature was needed to respond to them.

We should pause to identify one of the main charges leveled at Dewey by his opponents, an objection which persists to this day. His adversaries claimed that in initiating a highly pragmatic approach to education, the basic components of a classic education, such as history, literature, language and the arts, would be eliminated. Dewey disclaimed this assertion, in pointing out that the basic substance of classic learning must not be lost.

In short, the point I am making is that rejection of the philosophy and practice of traditional education sets a new type of difficult educational problem for those who believe in the new type of education. We shall operate blindly and in confusion until we recognize this fact; until we thoroughly appreciate that departure from the old solves no problems. [**] *. . . What avail is it to win prescribed amounts of information about geography and history, to win ability to read and write, if in the process the individual loses his own soul: loses his appreciation of things worthwhile, of the values to which these things are relative?* [***]

Dewey was clear that his objections to more classic studies arose not in what, but how, subject matter was taught.

How many came to associate the learning process with ennui and boredom? How many found what they did learn so foreign to the situations of life outside the school as to give them no power to control

*Cremin, *Traditions*, 55.
**Dewey, John. 1938. (12)
***Ibid., 50.

the latter? How many came to associate books with dull drudgery, so that they were "conditioned" to all but flashy reading matter.[*]

Seeking an emphasis to balance contemporary needs with classic learning is no easy matter. It seems apparent that Dewey, while never prescribing what this balance should be, suggests the need for an awareness on the part of the educator in making that decision himself.

It thus becomes the office of the educator to select those things within the range of existing experience that have the promise and potentiality of presenting new problems which by stimulating new ways of observation and judgment will expand the area of further experience. He must constantly regard what is already won not as a fixed possession but as an agency and instrumentality for opening new fields which make new demands upon existing powers of observation and of intelligent use of memory. Connectedness in growth must be his constant watchword.[**]

Chrissy McAllister teaches biology and botany at Principia College in Elsah, Illinois. Her classroom approach exemplifies the pragmatic and hands-on methods of Dewey. When not teaching on campus, she conducts her students on tours to New Zealand which she has found to be a rich area for direct learning. She leads her students in explorations of the mountains, beaches, and coastal waters of New Zealand, in gaining an awareness of the conservation challenges of that region. Her pupils return to the Illinois campus six to eight weeks later, brimming with the exhilaration of firsthand experience. Ms. McAllister's direct learning approach is a great favorite with the students.

Ms. McAllister gave an assignment recently to be explored

*Ibid., 15.
**Ibid., 90.

by her students: "What is a library?" Her methods raised eyebrows among her peers but her students came away from this exploration with far more than conventional knowledge. Colleagues were impressed. I questioned her about her approach:

RM: What did you do to help your freshman students learn about the library?

CM: This goes back to what we were talking about, that education works best when the students have some sort of enthusiasm about the topic, something they've got to bring to it. I didn't want to just bring them over to the library, to sit at the desks, to listen to the talks, that sort of thing. So I told them that they were going to do a silent tour of the library and they were not allowed to talk, and they were to bring pencils, notebooks and that's it, and I was going to bring them to different places and I may point at things, I may not, but that anywhere I stopped they were to write down observations, and not just anything they saw, but what they heard, what they smelled, what they felt—anything—and so we did that. We went all over. I took them down to all the nooks and crannies of the library, to the vaults in the basement, and we went through this little lounge area on the first floor where we have this hot chocolate machine and a coffee machine. We went to some of those remote space carrels[*] that are tucked back in the stacks . . . we went to every single floor and then when we were done I gave them twenty minutes or a half hour and I said, "Using the observations you took, create a poem." So they did this and then we met with the librarian who gave her standard presentation, and the students came with all kinds of questions. And we shared a couple of their poems. Some of them were very creative, some of them were a little sarcastic, some of them anthropomorphized the library into a living thing, it was very creative, but they had all kinds of questions. There were questions like "How many data bases are there?", and

*Small cubicles for private study.

73

"How do I log on?" And there were things like, "Why is there this huge vault in the basement?" And "What's in there?" They would have gone through four years at Principia and never even known it was down there, let alone think to ask questions about it. The librarian told <u>me later that they never had so many people sign up for study spaces in the library ever!</u>

RM: Things like the couches and the coffee machines and their "ownership" of the study carrels helped to narrow the distance between a "place to study" and the outside world.

CM: Yes. I wanted them to realize that it wasn't an intimidating place to go. It wasn't an outdated place to go. That, you know, it's OK to physically go to the library!

RM: And it seems that now the students for the first time were learning so many ways that they could use the library.

CM: Yes. And they were learning that not because they were listening. You see it's hard to listen if you're uninterested and you're not connected in some way. It wasn't that it worked for everybody, and there were still people who were going, "Nyeh, Library!" But at least they saw that the library was an interesting place.

RM: They became participants, rather than just passive listeners?

CM: Exactly. Yes!

RM: How did the librarian feel about all this?

CM: She told me that she had never had such a responsive and enthusiastic group before—<u>and a group with so many questions!</u>[*]

*Interview with Instructor Chrissy MacAllister, Elsah, Illinois, August 8, 2007.

74

The Westland School

The theories of Dewey have now influenced educators worldwide. Innovators such as Maria Montessori, Rudolf Steiner and Horace Mann were but some who were highly influenced by his methods. Many other schools and societies are also committed to similar programs emphasizing the child's emotional and spiritual development.

I was curious to know how a Dewey-based curriculum manages to blend its emphasis on contemporary studies in a way which will serve the student seeking entrance in a university whose standards might demand expertise of a more conventional nature. I sought the answer from the director of the highly respected Westland School in Sherman Oaks, California, an institution which is based upon the educational theories and methods of John Dewey. According to Director Janie Lou Hirsch, Westland has consistently developed "thoughtful and accomplished students who are readily received in America's major colleges and universities."[*]

Director Hirsch described the methodology of Westland as follows:

> *The younger children in my K-6 school may spend six weeks pursuing one subject, such as baking, fire fighting, or the study of trees in their neighborhood. Every possible aspect of the subject is explored in that period. With the older children, the curriculum can be life in ancient Greece. Here the history, geography, government, social customs, theatre and music will be taken up with a variety of teachers. Our faculty has 5 full-time instructors and 6 part-time assistants teaching a broad spectrum of academic subjects ranging from history, writing, music, and physical education.[**]*

[*]Janie Lou Hirsch, interview with author, August 1999.
[**]Janie Lou Hirsch, interview with author, August 19, 1999.

75

In this approach, we note a "laboratory" method in play. The student first researches the facts of a given subject. But this represents the mere point of departure for the Westland student. The emphasis from this point lies in entering, as far as is possible, into the simulated life of the given period or subject. In studying tribal life in the stone age, for example, the student, after digging out important facts, might then be led to fabricate the costumes of the given tribe, construct their dwelling places, light their fires, boil their water, perform their songs and dances, and bake their bread—no small assignment. Here is where elements such as ancient cave paintings (if one can't make it to Lascaux, there are always good pictures) can support such a project. In short, an effort is attempted to re-create what it must be like to participate in such a culture.

The Westland School, a private institution, was founded in 1949 by a group of parents who wanted an alternative to the conventional public education system. Director Hirsch explained that while the curriculum varies from year to year, whatever the object of focus, the pupil benefits from the particular focus of study with a large amount of "collateral information." There is no grading of the students in these exercises, who, guided by their professors joining in the learning experience with them, are motivated solely by their own enthusiasm and love of learning. This seems to be readily observable in an informative DVD on The Westland School.

Still curious to know exactly what a young student does in any given study program, I located eight-year-old Charlie Morse, a participant in the recent "Alaskan Studies" class, and asked him what he had learned. His reply:

We learned to make soapstone carvings and we made Inuksuk sculptures (large pieces). We learned to make finger masks of animals we studied. I studied the musk ox. We made an igloo of styrofoam."[*]

*Charlie Morse, telephone interview with author, July 27, 2004.

Charlie's mother, Libby, added helpful details:

For two months the children submerged themselves into the Inuit culture. They had to figure out engineering and architecture. Skin tents were hand sewn together and reinforced with barbecue skewers. The tents were adorned with sculpted talismen to look like bones. They substituted whipping cream for whale blubber. At the end, the other classes visited "Inuit City," and the culmination was the sharing of Inuit baked bread, and performing of Inuit songs and dances. [*]

Back to Charlie, who deserves the last word. "What are your final thoughts?" I asked.

"It taught me how they dressed and what they made," replied Charlie. "And it made me feel like I was an Inuit." (Plate 4). A pause, and then, "It was fun doing it." [**]

---

*Libby Morse, telephone interview with author, July 27, 2004.
**Ibid.

(Plate 4) Charlie Morse: in role as a native Alaskan Inuit. (Photo courtesy of Libby Morse)

Recapitulation of Achievements of Educational Pioneers

I have compressed much history in detailing some of the chief contributions that were to inspire the methods of the coming Theatre-in-Education Movement. Here is a brief summary:

Ancient Western Education

1. Learning took place in a highly controlled environment.

2. The student was a passive recipient.

3. One-way and mostly "once only" communication between instructor and student, usually in a lecture format.

4. Learning as a solemn duty.

5. An unquestioning approach on the part of the student.

6. The student at the periphery of the learning circle.

Reforms Since Rousseau

1. Learning takes place through contact with the outside world as a laboratory.

2. The student, guided by the instructor, takes initiative in the learning process.

3. Student and teacher share at each step in the acquisition of learning with adequate time to explore.

4. Learning through "play" in arousing a love of gathering knowledge.

5. An approach which encourages questioning, direct observation and experimentation.

6. The student and instructor sharing the center of the circle.

SIX

PIONEERS OF THE THEATRE-IN-EDUCATION MOVEMENT

On the final day of the 2000 conference of the American Association of Theatre in Higher Education, convened that year at Gallaudet University in Washington, D.C., a group of some thirty attendees were gathered in a conference room for a recapitulation discussion. The term "TIE," an acronym for Theatre-in-Education, had been bandied about considerably during four days, and a panel of TIE experts chaired by Chris Vine of New York University's Creative Arts Team were fielding questions. Some half-hour into the discussion a young woman who had attended an intense four days of meetings raised her hand tentatively and with a faint trace of apology asked, "Please, could you tell me what exactly *is* TIE?" A sympathetic bubble of laughter rippled around the conference room.

Once the title of a formal movement in Great Britain in the 1960's adopted by a group of educators known as the Coventry Group, Theatre-in-Education, (TIE) was the outgrowth of what was known as Drama in Education (DIE), or the first efforts to introduce theatre techniques into the British classroom for teaching purposes in the early days of the twentieth century. The aim from the outset was to utilize theatre techniques for the acquisition of knowledge. By now, in the early days of the 21st Century, TIE theory has expanded its methods to include a wide range of techniques, such as storytelling, musical theatre, dance, and writing of prose and poetry, and it is in this wider context that TIE will be employed in this book. In these methods and ever-expanding techniques, there is a unifying factor that identifies theatre-in-education practice, and that is theatre utilized for the purpose of acquiring knowledge.

It is important to understand that the focus of knowledge itself expanded greatly during the 18th and 19th Century, and especially after the industrial revolution. Social sciences, for example, gather information on our life habits, but more emphatically in the twentieth and early twenty-first century, the problems are prompted by an increasingly irresponsible society. The natural sciences are dedicated with urgency to reversing centuries of misuse of the earth's animal, vegetable and mineral resources. Social unrest producing crime and violence has also become a strong focus of education.

To respond to these factors the TIE movement has been undergoing a similar expansion. It recognizes, for one thing, that more than knowledge is needed to shape the responsible human being. Rediscovering what Plato and other early philosophers told us centuries ago, learning is now concerned with producing a morally responsible human being who will be capable of relating peacefully to others in contributing to a harmonious society.

Some social observers today point out, for one reason or another, that these initiatives are properly the business of a church, a civic group or an ecological society; others disagree, emphasizing that the cultivation of humane values can make little headway until supported by all of these, acting in conjunction with the family.

The arts cannot purport to provide the whole answer to this need for a more tolerant and kind society. But evidence now reveals that the arts, involved as they are with the creation of humane values of family feeling, inclusion, and beauty are capable of furthering the growth of social connectedness, and consequently with harmonizing life.

Harriet Finlay Johnson: Joy in the Learning Process
(DVD disc 1: section 2)

"Perhaps Sompting is the only village in England where the children cannot be kept out of school."[*]

Harriet Finlay Johnson (1871–1956) was the headmistress of the Sompting School, in West Sussex, Great Britain, and in 1897 was the first to employ drama techniques in the classroom. Identifying with the humane efforts of Rousseau, two centuries before, Finlay Johnson was committed to transforming the oppressive atmosphere of the classroom to one of enthusiasm and joy. She was a woman of sound scholarship, strong convictions and unshakable determination. She also possessed great courage and a dauntless romantic flair. In an age which frowned upon the idea of women as leaders, Finlay Johnson was the Jeanne d'Arc of the Theatre-in-Education movement (see plate 5) as she fearlessly and single-handedly planted the banner of drama for the first time into the potentially rich turf of the classroom.

Her story is passed down to us in two books: her own vivid account of her academic odyssey, *The Dramatic Method of Teaching,* published around 1911 (no publication date appears in the book), and a recent 2002 biography by Mary Bowmaker, *A Little School on the Downs.* Harriet Finlay Johnson's writing, in addition to detailing her classroom techniques, represents, like that of Rousseau, a call to action. Hear the distant echoes of Rousseauean trumpets!

Go forth, little book, from my halting pen, into the world of men and women of learning, knowledge, culture and research! Tell

---

*Johnson, *The Dramatic Method of Teaching*, 3.

(Plate 5) Harriet Finlay Johnson: the first teacher to utilize drama techniques for the purpose of imparting knowledge. (Photo courtesy of James Nesbit Publishers)

*them of the little school on the Sussex Downs where children and teachers lived for a space in the world of romance and happiness. Preach the gospel of happiness in childhood for those who will be the world's workers and fighters to-morrow. Bring home to your readers the conviction that fleeting childhood's days should be filled with joy.** *

Biographer Mary Bowmaker comments on the kind of daring required by a woman in the early days of the twentieth century in espousing such progressive methods.

*For young women, especially in those times, to make a stand alone, and go against the many practices in schools that had been perpetuated for generations required tremendous courage. And for the people of Sompting, young and old alike, to have the vision and find the "will" to support her and make the great experiment possible was admirable in itself.** ** *

Finlay Johnson was convinced that her 8–13-year-old students would express more enthusiasm for their studies and learn more effectively when drama replaced the conventional methods of lectures and discussion groups. Recorded from old manuscripts and letters, the Bowmaker biography provides much information on Finlay Johnson's classroom techniques and her personal life. Bowmaker's text, which is accompanied by rich pictorial documentation, conveys a clear, detailed sense of Finlay Johnson's innovative teaching methods as well as the expansive personal style that animated them. Remarkable photographs depict her students acting out great moments of history and also touching moments of her private life, such as her tender relationship with her husband, George Weller.

*Johnson, *Dramatic Method of Teaching*, 3.
**Bowmaker, *Little School on the Downs*, 17.

It was fortunate that Finlay Johnson was headmistress of the Sompting school and not required to obtain "board approval" for introducing her original methods. Theatre in the early 1900's was largely associated with the "naughtiness" of the Victorian music hall, and as such, drama, in the eyes of educational authorities, would never have passed muster as a suitable subject to be introduced to children. Add to this the suspect factor of "play," and an instructor, especially a woman, was confronting an academic Mt. Everest.

But Finlay Johnson's methods demonstrated from the outset a well-conceived logic. First of all, by leading her young students of twelve and thirteen years out of the classroom and into the fields and woods surrounding Surrey to record their own observations, she gave the children a liberating change from the rigidly set rows of the classroom. This hands-on method of learning was then transferred to other subjects, such as history, literature and the arts.

*The first aid which I invoked was Nature Study, mainly from its aesthetic standpoint, and from the very first I realized that, to be of any value, it must be Nature really studied by the child itself. It must not be Nature filtered though pictorial illustration, text-book, dried specimen and scientific terms, finally dribbled into passive children's minds minus the joy of assimilation; but it must be the real study of living and working Nature, absorbed in the open air under conditions which allow for free movement under natural discipline. And since Nature is the storehouse from which poet and artist draw their inspiration, it naturally follows that we found it but a brief step from the study of the open book of Nature to the Elysian fields of Literature and the Arts.**

*Johnson, The Dramatic Method of Teaching, 16.

85

The fact that Finlay Johnson's young pupils were soon learning more effectively and with more enthusiasm confirmed her theories.

> *A child learns, and retains what he is learning, better by actually seeing and doing things, which is a guiding principle of Kindergarten. There is not a very marked difference between the ages of the children who enjoy learning by Kindergarten games and the so-called "older scholars." Why not continue the principle of the Kindergarten game in the school for older scholars? I did so, but with this difference: instead of letting the teacher originate or conduct the play, I demanded that, just as the individual himself must study Nature and not have it studied for him, the play must be the child's own.* [*]

Because the play *was* the "child's own," the children took great pride and pleasure in it, and by 1900 Finlay Johnson was seeing that drama could arouse enthusiasm for *any* kind of subject matter. Children took great pleasure in learning the facts of history by these new methods which featured play, even if the demands on the students were much greater than those imposed by conventional learning methods. Not content with having her children consult a single source, Finlay Johnson imported multiple texts into the classroom, covering each subject under study. One has only to peruse the photographs of her students examining these texts and subsequently "acting out" historical scenes, as recorded in *The Dramatic Method of Teaching*, to get an impression of the unmistakable fun the children took in this learning process. Events such as the coronation of Sir Walter Raleigh, the death of Lord Nelson, Charles I bidding farewell to his family on the eve of his 1649 execution (Plate 6), a depiction of an early seventeenth century American Thanksgiving, and a Maori funeral ceremony, were all

*Ibid, 19.

(Plate 6) Finlay Johnson's class using theatre to teach history—shown here: Charles I bidding farewell to his family on the eve of his 1649 execution. (Photo courtesy of James Nesbit Publishers)

faithfully acted out with the support of period capes, crowns, hats, breeches and dresses, as well as swords, wagons, parchment and quill pens—*all* realized through in-depth research by these 8–13-year-old children. (see DVD version) This exercise in "collateral learning" developed by Finlay Johnson was to remain the hallmark of the Theatre-in-Education movement to our day.

Finlay Johnson's pupils were responsible for answering important questions about each scene. For instance, in the Charles I farewell to his family on the eve of his execution above, what must have been the emotions of the king's immediate family, his wife and children? Who among the court entourage were the king's defenders at this fateful moment? Who were his enemies? Imaginary dialog based on actual court records was created.

This thoroughness in developing believable characterizations recalls the sophisticated methods urged by leading world theatre directors of the 19th century. Directorial innovations of the German Duke of Meiningen and the renowned Russian theatre director and teacher, Constantin Stanislavsky come to mind. Both of these theatre innovators insisted that all actors, whether impersonating principal roles or playing the lowest member of the court, develop a strong familiarity with their character's background and motivations.[*]

As any innovator, Finlay Johnson had her detractors. Her adversaries claimed that these young students could not possibly carry out such a demanding program. The extensive research, the demands on the imagination in creating imaginary dialog, the fashioning of period costumes and props and the developing of period songs and dances —all this would place an impossible burden on these young pupils. But Finlay Johnson rejected all labels of inadequacy.

> *What struck me most forcibly always was the fact that nothing—the amount of preparation, the arrangement of multitudinous details, the memorizing of long, long parts, or the making of copious notes—ever seemed to be looked upon as the least trouble. . . .*
> *And even adults never confess to weariness when they want to do anything; pleasure unbalances the other sensations.*[**]

Harriet Finlay Johnson's conviction proved true. Learning became the source of joy, never of burden, for her students at the Sompting school, and it is recorded that these young pupils *insisted* on being in the classroom, often against the urging of par-

*These methods of dramatic preparation are described in detail by Constantin Stanislavsky in *Creating a Role* and *Building a Character.*
**Bowmaker, *Little School*, 111.

ents when facing health difficulties. Biographer Mary Bowmaker records this amusing item from the Sompting village newspaper:

> *One reporter, from the Morning Leader wrote: Perhaps Sompting is the only village in England where the children cannot be kept out of school.* [*]

Finlay Johnson, herself, observed how this love of learning is arrived at:

> *The joy of knowing the beauties of the living world around us and of probing its mysteries; the delights of finding sympathetic thoughts in the best of English literature (a literature unrivaled in the world!); the gradual appreciation of the beautiful in art; the desire which all these bring to burning youth to be up and "doing likewise"; the awakening of the young enthusiasm, even of merely evanescent youthful dreams, instead of the soul-deadening monotony and limitation of technical instruction—these are the things that count. Let the boy that delights in experiment and investigation follow his bent, and, when he himself is ready and eager for it, then supply the necessary technical instruction. Do not damp and kill the fires of young enthusiasm; they make the world go round.* [**]

TIE authority and historian Gavin Bolton elaborates on this factor of arousing the joy of learning, even in subjects that some might regard with downright boredom:

> *Dramatisation, Finlay Johnson claims, provides the means of "arousing a keen desire to know"; it was to be an incentive (my choice of word) to learning. Even the most unpalatable subject matters laid down by the school authorities could be taught*

*Ibid., 3.
**Johnson, Harriet Finlay. 1912. (13, 14)

through dramatisation, concealing, as Miss Johnson puts it, "the powder in the jam."[*]

Finlay Johnson is credited as the first teacher to utilize theatre methods in the classroom, and yet, but for the dates of her activity, one might be tempted to place her at the zenith of TIE achievement. *The Dramatic Method of Teaching* should occupy a favored place on the shelf of every educator.

There is a rather sad footnote to the life story of Harriet Finlay Johnson. She married a former student, George William Weller, fifteen years her junior. Though in no way an illicit relationship, she suffered acutely from the harsh judgement of her community. From 1910, Harriet Finlay Johnson was never again to set foot in the classroom. Harriet and George enjoyed a long and happy marriage, however, from 1910 to 1952, when George passed away.

H. Caldwell Cook
(DVD disc 1: section 3)

Unlocking the treasures and pleasures of Shakespeare

H. CALDWELL COOK (1886–1937), English Master at the prestigious Perse School for boys in Cambridge, England, and a contemporary of Finlay Johnson, was to utilize drama as a learning tool through a method called the "Direct Method of Learning."

Cook was master of a wide range of skills which included oral communication, choral singing, history, literature, poetry,

*Bolton, *Acting in Classroom Drama*, 10.

90

dance, music and the visual arts. He contended that during the years from 11 to 14, the young person possessed unlimited capacities for learning, and it was at this period that the child's exposure to classical training should begin.

Nowhere was this more convincingly demonstrated than in his teaching of Shakespeare. Cook insisted that the best way to *learn* Shakespeare was to *perform* him. The idea was instantly derided by the academic community of Perse, who insisted that these young students lacked the required background to understand Shakespeare's phrases and complex plots, let alone act them out. Cook's response, similar to that of Harriet Finlay Johnson, was that if the subject is made interesting, our young students are capable of performing whatever tasks with understanding and mastery. As with Finlay Johnson, the factor of play was the linchpin to learning.

> *"What shall we devise of equal power to claim the boys' serious interest, to gain their goodwill and enlist their whole-hearted co-operation? The answer is Play. The subjects to be learnt must be presented in an interesting way, and then the boys will have a natural desire to do the work. That is how you enlist their co-operation in the classroom."*[*]

Cook was a man possessed of an impassioned love of theatre. This tall and imposing figure dressed in his perennial Oxford blazer (Plate 7) would frequently be observed striding through the fields of Perse sharing his love of poetry with his boys. Cook's classroom featured a "mummery," or small theatre space, which became the "*champs de bataille*" (the boys adored dressing in "armor" and carrying shields and swords!) on which the struggles for

---

*Beacock, *Play Way English for To-day*, 13.

**(Plate 7) H. Caldwell Cook: creator of the "The Play Way,"
(Photo credit: Thomas Nelson & Sons Publishers)**

(Plate 8) Caldwell Cook's class in motion: the only way to learn Shakespeare is to perform him. (Photo credit: Thomas Nelson & Sons Publishers)

power and lovers' trysts would capture the minds of his students. (Plate 8)

In this "direct learning" approach, the early teenagers might be observed struggling to maintain their balance on the "Mummery" floor as they transported unwieldy volumes of Shakespeare texts in the beginning steps of creating a scene. It was slow going at first as the boys were asked to stop whenever it became necessary to look up a word or phrase in the rear of the volumes, or to consult the Shakespeare Variorium edition which was always at hand. With each repetition of a scene, however, the momentum of the action would mount, until eventually, the young actors would "own" the text and the big books would be gradually laid aside as real acting began.

When invited into Cook's classroom to witness a performance, the attitude of the "scoffers" changed dramatically. It was magical to them, as observer and biographer D.A. Beacock, himself an early skeptic, observed. He and others witnessed compelling productions of *Julius Caesar, The Merchant of Venice, Henry IV, Part One, Henry V, Twelfth Night* and *Hamlet*. These skeptical visitors were utterly astonished, not only by the high quality of the acting, but also at what the boys had *learned* about the plays of Shakespeare. Beacock observes:

> *When, therefore, Caldwell Cook devoted a couple of periods at the end of each term to an ingenious system of context-chasing to test the Form's knowledge of the text, it was a pleasant surprise to me to see how much of the play they had obviously understood. It was apparent to me that a more thorough appreciation of the play was achieved than by the old dull methods, and that the association of the words with sound and action had impressed the lines far more firmly on the boys' memories.* [*]

Cook was not concerned with teaching for the standard "test scores," (roughly the equivalent of the American SAT business), but only with developing the intellectual and moral culture of his students. Superintendent Beacock elaborates:

> *Caldwell Cook had little use for the School Certificate Examination, or for the kind of teaching it required. It has been left to others to see how far his methods can find a place in the curriculum of a modern secondary or public school, where examination needs have to be considered. It is true that a boy often has to be taught not what will benefit him most but what examiners insist upon his knowing. In most houses the demand of the parents to-day is not for the culture of mind or development of character, so much as for*

*Ibid., 59–60.

the immediate potentiality of earning a living. Many teachers, therefore, are unable to adopt Caldwell Cook's methods in toto, and consequently reject them altogether.[*]

Other proofs of the efficacy of Cook's methods were the successes of his students, who confirmed these results years later in many letters to their beloved teacher. One former student wrote:

I count myself exceedingly fortunate that it was under Caldwell Cook's guidance that I was first introduced to the plays of Shakespeare. My early memories of the greatest imaginative works in our tongue have nothing to do with fussy notes and irritating pedantry. We read the plays in a good plain text, with nothing at the back but a Glossary where we could find the meaning of difficult words. If there were occasional phrases that eluded us, what did that matter? For this was not a book to be studied, but a play to be acted. We wore cloaks and hats, we flourished swords and daggers, and the play escaped from the bondage of the print in which it was confined and became again the darling child of Shakespeare's fancy. Even from those crude, childish presentations, when actors spoke with one eye on the audience and the other on their text, I have recollections of beauty or drama which are at the roots of my love for Shakespeare.[**]

And Beacock summarizes:

. . . however searching the criticism may be—and he sometimes shirked the issues involved—yet he had one last line of defense. His logic can be assailed, his theories ridiculed , but he could always point to the solid results that he achieved. These cannot be lightly dismissed.[***]

---

[*]Ibid., 102.
[**]Ibid., 116.
[***]Ibid., 102.

The "direct learning" approach to Shakespeare enjoys a delightful and moving modern counterpart in an account recorded in Jonathan Kozol's 1991 volume, *Savage Inequalities*, where the author tells the story of a teenage boy from an environmentally tough New York neighborhood. His name was Carlos, and he was headed for academic disaster. His salvation came one day when he randomly picked up a copy of Shakespeare. The ensuing events were witnessed by Jack Forman, head of the English Department at New York City's Morris High:

> *I have strong feelings about getting past the basics. Too many schools are stripping down curriculum to meet the pressure for success on tests that measure only minimal skills. That's why I teach a theater course. Students who don't respond to ordinary classes may surprise us, and surprise themselves, when they are asked to step on a stage.*
>
> *I have a student, Carlos, who had dropped out once and then returned. He had no confidence in his ability. Then he began to act. He memorized the part of Pyramus. Then he played Sebastian in The Tempest. He had a photographic memory. Amazing! He will graduate, I hope, this June.*
>
> *Now, if we didn't have that theater program, you have got to ask if Carlos would have stayed in school.*[*]

It may baffle the reader, as it did biographer Beacock, how an academic community could quarrel with Cook's overall results. I take the liberty of quoting a moving excerpt from another former student destined to become one of England's finest twentieth century actors:

> *Dear Mr. Caldwell Cook,*
> *   As I write, you are standing facing me, tall and smiling, and I*

*Kozol, *Savage Inequalities*, 101–102.

have become very small, about the size of a boy in the Second Form. To say what you have meant to me during twenty years—this is a strange and difficult task. . . .

It is as though I was standing with you in a great hall, with many closed doors, and you had unlocked the doors one by one, and I had gone through into lighted passages. . . .

That is how it seems to me now, but it was not like that then; then there was nothing surprising in finding new things; they appeared without one's making any effort. When I was about ten years old, you dangled me on a piece of rope in the water, and I discovered that I could swim; after that I trusted you implicitly; that was why discoveries made with you did not seem disturbing. Today I was reading a poem and couldn't understand it. "Where is the beat?" I asked myself. I soon found how the rhythm went; then the meaning became clear. I discovered that method, of course, with you, twenty years ago when you conducted the class with a musician's baton—do you remember?

Oh, to remember all the new thoughts and notions which thronged my brain at that time! What did the Moors really look like?—Find out by trying to dress up like them in the Tiring House! Who was Portia's father, Cato?—Find out by looking in the big, black Plutarch! This punctuation in Macbeth is strange!—Compare it with the facsimile First Folio on the top shelf! Shaw is a clever man, isn't he?—Third shelf from the bottom! I wish I could write a really good short story!—Take Saki home with you!—Oh, the London theatre is wonderful!—Really? If you have an hour to spare, take a look at this book—Gordon Craig's The Theatre Advancing. "My little toy casket the Mummery," as you once sadly called it, was a treasure house for us, a treasure house of ideas, many of which we couldn't understand—but that didn't matter! If The Theatre Advancing and King Lear were put back on the shelves uncut, we remembered that they were there to be taken out, years later perhaps, their pages patiently waiting to be sliced open.

That we were able to live those days we owed not only to you, but to Dr. Rouse. Dr. Rouse once told me that you were a genius, and he repeated: "Mind you, I mean, Genius!" He knew that from you we were receiving true education. Spending those many hours in search and experiment in the Mummery did not bring us nearer to the School Certificate and its dreaded "set-books." How right Dr. Rouse was to "let be." I can only judge now when I think how little I remember of the School Certificate, set-books and how much I can remember of your books in the Mummery.

We often met and talked after I left the Perse; but my last clear memory of you was in the Mummery on a winter's evening. You will not remember, for you did not know that I was watching you. We were acting Antony and Cleopatra and the lines were spoken;

Unarm, Eros; the long day's task is done,
And we must sleep.

Your eyes were far away, floating in tears, but your lips were smiling: I think I understood Tragedy for the first time then; as I looked at you, you seemed to say: "Oh, my profound heart!" You have that look on your face now as you stand before me; it is as clear as fifteen years ago; now your face is changing, it is smiling.

Well, Sir, I have tried to remember, to crystallize and set down; although I have done it inadequately, at least you know that I am now, as I always was,

Your most grateful and affectionate pupil,

Marius Goring. [*]

It is recorded that Cook never accepted a penny for his teachings, but lived only to bring the inspiration of beauty, language and the love of poetry to his pupils.

Cook suffered serious wounds in World War I which left him shell-shocked. He never completely recovered. He became more and more of a recluse, but of those last years, we know certain de-

---

*Beacock, *Play Way English for To-Day*, 118–122. Excerpts from a letter to Caldwell Cook from Marius Goring, who was to become a leading 20th Century British stage and film actor.

tails. Beacock records that by 1931 his nerves had become so frayed that he was unable to return to teaching.

Under these changed conditions he grew depressed, and lacked the incentive to carry on his work. His early enthusiasm withered as he perceived popular disregard of most of the ideals he had formerly cherished. [*]

His health declined until 1937 when he entered a nursing home with the greatest reluctance. He passed away on Wednesday, May 17th of that year. He was 53 years of age.

His funeral was attended by his family, many of his associates, admirers and friends. It is recorded that few of the journals which had formerly praised Cook, noticed his passing. M.D. Brown, a former student of Cook, writes:

He gave us an ear for words, an eye for words, a feel for words. He showed us expression and more than words meaning things. He revealed it as something alive, pulsing, breaking, surging. I can still remember how we wagged our little batons to "Come unto these yellow sands"—was it childish, ineffectual? I believe if I set myself now to analyze and appreciate that miraculous lyric, all I could say would be built upon what I can hear and feel of the infinitely subtle movement and rhythm of it, its modulations and resolutions, crescendos and cadences. It was in the Second Form that I began to listen.

His was a quality of insight little short of genius, expressing itself in graciousness, creating a new way of unveiling our newly opened eyes. It was a grasp of right ends that made right means.

All we can offer is our gratitude. [**]

[*]Ibid., 96.
[**]Brown, M.D., as quoted in Beacock, 123–124.

For Cook it seems that the moon was too near: he reached for the stars.

Peter Slade
(DVD disc 1: section 4)

Spontaneity at the Heart of Learning and Healing

British actor and teacher PETER SLADE (1912–2004) explored vital new fields that established him as one of the most influential educators of the 20th Century. He has ushered in new theatre teaching methods worldwide through his lectures and books, notably *Child Drama* and *Experience of Spontaneity*, both of which have been translated into many languages. Beyond devising his instruction techniques, he became increasingly moved by the needs of young people who suffered speech and other disabilities, and his healing methods led to his place as the acknowledged father of drama therapy.

In his early twenties, Slade was fascinated by the spontaneous movements of poor children playing in the streets of London. He would note the abrupt bursts of energy, the return to sudden stillness, and surprising reversion to acceleration—all motivated by unpredictable forces producing excitingly musical, and significant patterns of behavior. Slade saw these patterns as pure drama.

Child Drama is an art form in its own right; it is not an activity that has been invented by someone, but the actual behavior of human beings . . . and because the root of Child Drama is play, it is with play that we must largely concern ourselves in the first instance.[*]

*Slade, *Experience*, 1.

100

Carefully detailed observations found in his book, *Child Drama*, analyze the behavior of the child with a thoroughness unrivaled to this day.

This pursuit of spontaneity which Slade called "individuation, " formed the basis of all his therapeutic work with young and mature people in workshops in all corners of the United Kingdom. Slade's preoccupation with spontaneity dated from school experiences as a teenager. In these early years, he would improvise dramatic events with his fellow students, where fantasy blended with reality, and history with myth for hours and days on end. These spontaneous gambols would wind through the streets of London or upwards on alpine slopes in a kind of science fiction celebration of life. Slade describes these imaginative excursions:

> *Other things we danced were the stories and myths of ancient Greece . . . Sometimes we spoke, but mostly we had no breath for it. The form of work was in itself a strenuous form of training, and at the same time a remarkable opportunity for acting out deeply, not only our own griefs, but the griefs and joys of the gods themselves in the great stories of the World. I look back upon that dancing as something, which instilled into me once and for all the deep knowledge of the standards of the effort and beauty which have been my yardstick since, in the judging of professional and amateur work of every kind. Such dance as this was, many years later, to form the basic training for the Pear Tree Players, and other professional companies that have asked my aid.* [*]

Peter Slade formed his first theatre troupes in 1931 and in 1932, and this period produced *The Children's Theatre Company*. Though his lifetime base remained in Birmingham, England, he would eventually travel the world in demonstrating and sharing

*Ibid., 43.

his original techniques of child education. I am fortunate to have known some of those who have worked with Slade; the experience must have been remarkable.

As Slade explains, transformational results with children first came about through what he termed "natural dance," pioneered through the years with his wife, Sylvia Demmery. Natural dance allowed the child's inner feelings to surface in releasing buried feelings. Spontaneous movement patterns would eventually merge with an equally spontaneous approach to language, referred to by Slade as "language flow." It was completely unnecessary that either the language or the movement translated into recognizable sense, the objective being simply to release the emotions.

One should add that spontaneity is such a remarkable thing that it is possible for people to hold conversations in foreign tongues yet catch a deep sympathy and understanding.[*]

Theatre educator Gavin Bolton, a longtime observer and associate of Slade, records that the word "drama," for Slade, best described "The Art of Living," and he adds:

It is the shared unconscious achievement of a group of children who spontaneously create "moments of theatre" that mark Slade's approach as an art.[**]

Here is an example of an exercise where movement and "language flow" merge, as recorded in *Experience of Spontaneity.* It entails a narrative entitled, *Two Dolphins, Caliban and a Whale,* roughly based on Shakespeare's *The Tempest,* and consists of a recreation of an imaginary sea journey and the need to survive a

[*]Ibid., 52.
[**]Bolton, *Classroom Drama*, 148.

perilous shipwreck. The action was accompanied by music, a device often used by Slade in sensitizing his students to the atmosphere of an event. In this case, the impressionistic music of Debussy's *La Mer* accompanied the exercise in evoking the movements of the sea. Free movement also encouraged spontaneous verbal associations.

> *The Shakespeare lines, "The clouds methought would open and show riches," provoked the question, "What sort of riches?" Answers came: "Money, toffees, food, beer, chocolates, chance to go home to Mother."*

This "free association" of speech with improvised movement turned out to represent a vital combination in unlocking the latent impulses of his young actors. This method of "free flow" in language and movement also influenced theatre educators to follow, such as David Booth, who will be discussed in the next chapter.

Slade consulted closely with the medical profession as he worked extensively with disabled children in forming his own clinic. His 1947 election to the City of Birmingham's Education Committee established him as an authority on healing through drama, and his successes in this field provided him with a forum throughout the British Isles and in many foreign lands.

Slade was to point out that the staid and mechanized approach to drama education then popular in English schools, must itself be challenged. The emphasis on improvisation and free behavior stood in strong opposition to conventional and "set" methods of drama training. Of course there was great adversity among the drama teachers of the day. To comprehend why, it is necessary to understand that the prevailing methods of theatre training in the 1930's and 40's in the United Kingdom were rooted in

*Slade, *Experience*, 89–96.

103

long-established speech and movement conventions. These manu-factured conventions designed to *illustrate* emotion, rather than *having it,* served to deny the student's authentic feelings. In speech, for example, England's children were being trained in an Oxbridgian, or a BBC-oriented tradition, demanding strict adher-ence to established patterns. Students were advised from their ear-liest lessons when to lift the voice, when to pause, and how to illustrate emotional stress. The same mechanized approach gov-erned corporeal expression. Predetermined gestures, which we might liken to a "semaphore" system, would appropriately express "fear," "sorrow" or "elation." If the young theatre student could repeat these predetermined speech and movement patterns profi-ciently, he or she would draw high marks.[*]

Slade was the first to challenge these highly manipulative methods which only served to crush out the child's authentic im-pulses. Slade's stress on the creation of inner truth was currently being introduced by the great Russian teacher, Constantin Stanislavsky, who surely must have influenced him.

Objections to Slade's liberating methods were ubiquitous. A major protest centered around the question of control. Permitting the child his free expression could only lead to chaos, claimed Slade's adversaries. Slade responded:

Certainly not—that is anarchy, not freedom, and does not lead to happiness.[**]

These objections to the freeing of spontaneous impulses in

*One sees evidence of this approach to acting in the Hollywood films of the 1920's which featured highly stylized gestures, often influenced by the Swiss Rudolf Laban, who devel-oped a fixed gesture vocabulary.
**Slade, *Sponteneity,* 22.

developing a performance were often persuasively answered when objectors to Slade's methods would visit his classes. One such observer was Mr. Martin Browne, Director of the British Drama League, initially a staunch opponent of Slade. After observing one of Slade's teaching sessions, Brown became an instant convert to his methods, and remarked, "I have only seen space used so perfectly before by first class ballerinas."[*]

Another fear of encouraging spontaneous behavior was that disunity would ensue. A longtime adversary of Slade, a high-ranking school official—humorously referred to by Slade as the "Dark One!"—also paid a visit to one of Slade's classes and remarked:

> *We've never seen anything like this before. I should never have believed it possible. It is the first time some of those lads have really cooperated and they were never out of control.*[**]

To this day, the relationship between freedom and control is still debated. Many of our training institutions for young actors still call for a fixed "result"—as opposed to a process which depends upon inner exploration. Slade's signal achievement was to create a harmonious balance between spontaneity and form, in which each cooperated comfortably in the development of a satisfying performance.

In an effort to protect the child's access to spontaneous behavior, Slade insisted that the child should not, during the stages of beginning training, be permitted to perform onstage, and, for similar reasons, not be enrolled in one of the training studios where conventional theatre techniques were operative. Premature stage appearances entailing the inevitable temptation to court audience

---

[*]Slade, *Experience*, 22.
[**]Ibid., 96.

approval could only serve to divide the young actor's concentration, distort truthful behavior, and produce a shallow performance.

These objections to conventionally accepted methods led to Slade's being labeled as "anti-theatre," but Slade who had played Shakespeare at the Old Vic, explained away this accusation:

> *To offer children other experiences than that of being on a raised proscenium stage is not in the least to say that one is against all theatre—a thing I have often been accused of. Indeed in later reports it may slowly appear that it is not only the child and his supreme spontaneous actions one attempts to guard, but because one's own standard of what the art of theatre ought to be is fierce and high, so one sees the primitive and unformed attempt as unacceptable. There are so many important in-between stages as part of life that ought to be experienced.*[*]

Peter Slade's gift to theatre education is inestimable. His insistence on the need for "individuation," or the respect for the child's natural impulses, have contributed to the reform of ancient and conventionally established theatre techniques in Britain and America. In addition, his methods emphasizing spontaneous behavior have served to heal untold numbers of handicapped children and adults.

Describing his healing experiences, Slade writes:

> *My mind immediately sees groups of students in innumerable training colleges, women's clubs, a group of police, service units, monks, many nuns, old men's clubs, mental patients, sad withered little children in hospitals, gay brave people "dancing" in wheel chairs, blind people "seeing" gardens to Debussy, deaf people "hearing" jazz to their finger beats and footsteps, people with no arms "juggling" with clubs, a particular bunch of directors of in-*

*Ibid., 19.

dustry, young actors, young outlaws, nurses, groups in community centers, many teachers from different lands and of course, so many children—they pass in a sort of filmic cavalcade as I write. [*]

On June 30, 2004, at a London memorial service honoring Peter Slade, the words of Dr. John Dodd suggest the depth of Slade's contribution to education and humanity.

Peter Slade was a great man because he cared about those less fortunate and worked tirelessly to create and promote a way of working that will benefit future generations of children and adults.

Dorothy Heathcote

The infinite inventiveness of the theatre educator

Dorothy Heathcote (1926–) is a highly influential pioneer of TIE theory and teacher. To this day, her work has been centered in her native Durham in the United Kingdom, though she has also expanded the uses of drama for learning worldwide. As recently as in the summer of 2007, she was teaching workshops in her technique sponsored by the Creative Arts Team at New York University. Heathcote possesses a boundless knowledge of history, science, the arts and human behavior, and her knowledge of life, past and present, is so vast, and her intuition so developed, that many consider her technique inimitable. This is true in the sense that the manner in which she develops a workshop is unique to her remarkable talents. But we must come to look upon the methodology of Dorothy Heathcote not as a model to be imitated—an impossible

*Ibid., 243.

107

task—but rather as an encouragement to any educator attracted to her methods. Heathcote's approach has influenced many who have borrowed elements from it, and this is as it should be; artists are no less artists for honoring the influences which have inspired their own originality. The world of art is rife with examples: Mozart, however influenced by his model, does not remain Haydn, and Giotto, whom Kenneth Clark cites as an unmatched Renaissance genius, springs from the originality of Duccio.

Prominent among Heathcote's innovative methods is what she terms "The Mantle of the Expert." In this approach, the teacher will serve as a collaborator and guide to her students in the course of a theatre study, which can evolve over a period of days or weeks. In the role of "the Expert," Heathcote may play herself in interrupting the development of the story, or go "in role" in playing a character who suddenly "appears." These "appearances" serve to urge a deeper reflection on the unfolding events, or simply to move the plot forward with more relevance. This intervention, or kind of "stop action" in the course of creating a dramatic event, is designed to allow the actors the opportunity to reflect on their choices of behavior and to contemplate more productive alternatives. With Heathcote, then, theatre is not conceived in conventional terms of creating a performance. Rather, the drama is a means to inspire contemplation, learning and self-development.

Dorothy Heathcote may lead her students in exercises which delve into distant history or which treat contemporary events. In attending a 1972 workshop given by this remarkable teacher in Cleveland, Ohio, we watched a video of an exercise that took place over several days with a group of boys from a tough district in the UK, treating the recent assassination of the American president, John Kennedy.

In the course of attempting to recreate the events of the assassination in order to identify the guilty party, there would be pauses to allow the participants an opportunity to reflect which paths might be fruitful and which useless.* Then, at a given point, Heathcote would step completely out of the picture in allowing the uninterrupted scene to be played out.

I shall never forget the moment when the chief investigator eventually discovered the guilty party, the objective of the exercise. A young man, convinced that he had his man, turned toward the culprit, and then beckoned him to step forth with a gesture of chilling power. Yes, Dorothy Heathcote's pupils acquire acting skills as well.

What had the boys learned in process of performing this exercise? They had, through extensive research over a period of many weeks, gained insights into the background of President Kennedy and the facts leading to his election to the presidency; the social climate in America in those days which included the civil rights movement; the current paranoia on the subject of Communism; the life and activities of Lee Harvey Oswald and his sympathies with the Soviet Union; forensic evidence leading to the "Grassy Knoll" theory representing a conspiracy; American jurisprudence; of the rush to judgment which produced the Tower Commission report, and so on.

Here is the account of another exercise which is recorded in her 1995 volume, *Drama for Learning*, an excellent source for those seeking knowledge of Heathcote's methodology. This sequence was actually carried out by Marianne Heathcote, the

*Augusto Boal, the remarkable Brazilian theatre innovator of late 20th century also encouraged intervention in the course of an unfolding drama to allow for this same kind of reflection. His invention of "the Joker" parallels the role of "the Expert," of Heathcote, and one can read about his methods in his *Theatre of the Oppressed.*

daughter of Dorothy, and is an example of how Heathcote's methods might be successfully adapted by another.

The objective was to gain knowledge about life in Medieval France. To achieve this, the subject of the life of monks inhabiting a monastery was selected. Faced with the task of teaching "medieval history" to a group of ten to twelve-year-old students, Marianne Heathcote reflects:

As far as I could see, I had two options: the students could read some books from the library service collection and make notes and pictures from them about life in a medieval monastery, or they could behave as if they were real monks running a monastery and then, in role, write about how life in the monastery is. [*]

The dramatic event that would drive this search was the need to design a new scriptorium, or study, commissioned by the local Bishop Anselme. Roles were assigned to the students who then familiarized themselves with the tasks of maintaining a medieval monastery. These included:

Cellarers, Keeper of relics, Refectorians, Chamberlains, Almoners, Master of Novices, Infirmarian, Psalmist; Herbalist and Gardeners; Kitcheners; Flockmaster; Guardmaster; Sacristans; Precentors. [**]

Dramatic tension was provided by the arrival of a letter from a fictional Bishop Anselme who had an urgent need for the creation of this scriptorium. Here are some details of monastery life which had to be mastered by the ten to twelve-year-old students:

a detailed knowledge of the operation, duties and laws of the mon-

*Heathcote, *Drama for Learning*, 75.
**Ibid., 76.

astery including an acquaintance with the life of the monks, their schedules of worship and the ritual of their daily lives;

a demonstrable knowledge of the music of the period chanted at religious services;

how to bake the bread necessary for the sustenance of the monastery's inhabitants;

techniques of creating period vellum, quill pens and writing in medieval script form in order to respond to the Bishop;

the geography of the monastery, its architecture, including the consideration of adequate light to permit daily work in the new scriptorium.[*]

Was this enterprise feasible? Could the monks even *consider* accomplishing all this within a few short weeks to meet the Bishop's demands? Estimated schedules had to be devised, taking into account the required supplementary working hours if the monks were to complete the project. Could the monks come in under budget with the predetermined and limited funds available to them? The achievement of the scriptorium would lead to revenue desperately needed to repair the deteriorating bell tower and the aviary. A heated debate took place among the members of the order.

From the conception and scope of this exercise, one can grasp the enormous breadth of learning demanded of these children.

Respected TIE authority and author, Cecily O'Neil, suggests what is unique about the methods of this iconic teacher:

---

*Ibid., 15.

The significance of the social dimension of this kind of teaching should not be overlooked. Learning occurs most efficiently within a supportive and collaborative community. Here, students work in the kind of teams and collaborative environments that anticipate the challenges facing them in the real world. Instead of sterile competitiveness, everyone's level of achievement is elevated. The mantle of the expert sets up a supportive, interpretative, and reflective community through a pattern of relationships and a network of tasks, all embedded in a flexible context. . . . From the firm foundation provided by the teacher, the students gradually begin to take control of the imagined context they have helped to create. They <u>become</u> *experts—experts at learning.*[*]

The wide variety of highly original methods pioneered by Harriet Finlay Johnson, H. Caldwell Cook, Peter Slade and Dorothy Heathcote, opened wide the gates of creative teaching and learning for their followers today, as we shall observe in the next chapter.

*O'Neil, Cecily, from Foreword in *Drama for Learning*, viii, ix.

SEVEN

EXPANDING APPROACHES:
NEW LEADERS, NEW PATHS

Theatre educators, however influenced by the techniques of others, invariably utilize methods which have evolved from their own individual practice. The following interviews with highly effective teachers and directors are intended to suggest the wide range of these methods.

Meade Palidofsky
(DVD disc 1: section 5)

Unlimited ways to help our young people

"You see people from all different gangs suddenly becoming best friends, and if they were on the streets, they'd be shooting each other!"

—Meade Palidofsky

Motivated by the desire to help young people escape harsh social conditions in the Chicago area, Meade Palidofsky has worked in a wide variety of teaching methods which have included the writing of poetry, stories, plays and developing musical theatre. After graduation from the University of Michigan in the early

113

70's, she began writing plays and conducting playwriting workshops, and became active in political campaigns, as she says, "Just so I could feel that I was doing something." The desire to effect social change has continued to motivate her work ever since.

A high priority has always been bringing peace to the lives of young people in a disturbed society. She has observed her students overcoming the harsh effects of drug abuse and gang violence, and is now witnessing these students helping others along these same lines.

"When my husband, Alan Neff, and I decided to stay in Chicago instead of following an earlier desire to move to New York, I realized that I must focus on the work I wanted to do," she remarked in a 1998 Chicago interview. She formed the Chicago Dance Center, the Chicago Dramatic Workshop and the Chicago Dance Ensemble before becoming founding director of Chicago's Music Theatre Workshop for gifted students in 1984.

Many of Palidofsky's workshops, such as one she has directed at the Casa Atzlan in Chicago's impoverished Piltsin district, employ dramatization of the teenagers' own stories. The aim is to help lift young people from destructive habits by discovering alternative life options.

I started to write plays about what kids were really concerned about. We connected with community agencies and during this collaboration, I got interested in the group process, actually using the process of writing a play to think about their lives, you know, about what they were doing and what was going on, and I started doing that at the Juvenile Detention Center. And that I think is a really interesting process. You know the process of doing a show really brings people together. And if you actually do it around issues that people think about or need to think about. Well, what happens at the detention center is that you see people from all different gangs suddenly becoming best friends, and if they were on the street, they'd be shooting each other! And you see them transcend their gang lines and it becomes about doing the show and

114

*that becomes more important than the fact that they're all in differ-
ent gangs. So that idea became really important.*[*]

Palidofsky's current schedule also takes her to the high security Cook County Juvenile Detention Center where she oversees
writing and performing classes as part of prisoner rehabilitation.
On a blustering cold rainy day in February, 1998, I accompanied
Meade as she drove miles out of her way to visit her cast of boys at
the "Center." She had been detained by a business meeting and
though a rehearsal was no longer possible, she nevertheless considered it essential to reach these young men. Raising her voice in
order to be heard over the teeming rain on the windshield, she said,
"These boys have seen so much deception in their elders, and so
much disappointment, we must regain their trust."

In the detention center program, students sign a contract
which states that the participants will abstain from both violence
and profanity. When objections were raised by some of the young
inmates on the latter issue, Meade convinced them that "it is possible to find a more imaginative language than that commonly heard
in the streets." One boy, Ernie, an embryonic poet whose writing
featured an abundant number of four letter words, protested
strongly. But respecting his director's judgment, he eventually
came up with lines such as these:

*"We sell the drugs without hesitation, Dipping our hands into the
pot of devastation."*

I followed Meade Palidofsky on a long walk through the anti-
septically waxed hallways of the Juvenile Detention Center. The
journey conducting her to one after another of her actors was a
moving lesson in commitment.

*Palidofsky: Chicago interview with the author, April 12, 1998.

The Music Theatre Workshop

Meade Palidofsky's *Music Theater Workshop* is meant for a different segment of young people. This group includes gifted high school students from the Chicago public school system, chosen through an audition process. In the winter of 1998 I attended a rehearsal of their production, *Faces of Faith; a Dramatic Journey Through Origins and Beyond.* The production was a multi-disciplinary theatre piece designed to support the Chicago Field Museum's current exhibit on the evolution of mankind. Work for this ambitious project began during the summer of 1997 when the group researched a diversity of faith and belief systems. To gain understanding of these, the cast members interviewed a wide range of indigenous youth from Canada and Ireland; also adult survivors of the Holocaust, Muslim immigrants and many others.

The project was a striking example of "theatre in education." The students were called upon to master techniques of acting, dance, mime, creative writing, costume design and even the playing and creating of period musical instruments of various cultures and historical periods. Three weeks before the performance, I was allowed to observe rehearsal sessions with the group. Training sessions in movement and choral work were professionally conducted by choreographer and dancer Cheri D. Green, and choral director Claudia Howard Queen.

During a rehearsal break, I followed some of the kids into the lobby where six of them were sprawled near a soft drink machine. Dressed in their sweat suits and necks wrapped in colored towels, it was a scene reminiscent of relaxing actors of the Broadway, or any other, stage. I asked if they would discuss what performing in a theatre ensemble meant to them, and found them willing to share their thoughts.

Stefanie: *I feel a sense of pride for the first time.*

116

Becky: *Yes, this work boosts your confidence and makes you more mature.*

Ariste: (a recent émigré from her native Lithuania): *This experience has helped with my speech which was difficult coming from a foreign country. I also feel like I have made friends and found a family.*

Becky: *Yes, that's what we all feel, that we are a family.*

Gary: *Yeah, when the rehearsals are over a lot of the time, we just stay and talk together sometimes for hours. It's really like a new family.*

As with young participants in many other theatre workshops, "family" was the term heard most frequently.

The opening show of the Music Theatre Workshop event was performed to perfection. Meandering from room to room of the exhibit like an elegant serpent and carrying their strolling public with them in dramatizing the periods of history, from the stone age to modern times—through poetry, movement and dance—the performers enthralled a large audience.

In January of 2004, I again interviewed Meade Palidofsky. She was participating in four added Chicago area workshops including The Cook County Detention Center, the Illinois Youth in Warrenville, and The Peace Academy (collaborating with Genesis at the Crossroads)—a performing group which unites a wide variety of backgrounds, including Jews, Arabs, Bosnians, Pakistanis, Mexicans, and Puerto Ricans. In these workshops, issues such as prejudice, bullying and violence are explored to be healed.

I asked Meade what had prepared her to master her wide variety of techniques.

MP: My school has mainly been the streets. I studied plays. I observed in courtrooms. I interviewed a lot of kids. I asked a lot of questions. In the end, it's a matter of asking the right questions.

RM: From the vantage point of six years since we last talked, could you discuss any details of the evolution of the Musical Theatre Workshop?

MP: Well, what is great about it all is that we are seeing many kids formerly in the program now conducting and leading rehabilitation programs on their own! They are becoming the mentors of the next generation.

RM: Tell me more about the prison work.

MP: I correspond regularly with the boys and girls. The program has inspired them to read and write—and to make something of themselves. The authorities now have gained a respect for us through the changes they've witnessed in the kids. The big thing is they've actually dropped the association with gangs. And now these kids are actually teaching others in the prison!"

And, Meade exclaims in grateful delight, "the kids are actually *getting out!*"[*]

*Interview with the author, January 22, 2004.

Sherry and Bob Jason of City Hearts
(DVD disc 1: section 6)

Leading from darkness to light

"In 1977, as a new attorney, I toured Los Angeles Central Juvenile Hall where I watched in sadness and fascination as a convicted thirteen-year-old murderer took his first piano lesson. He was a prodigy, the music of Mozart touching his soul. I wondered what would have happened if he had met the piano before he met the gangs."

—Sherry Jason

City Hearts is described in its brochure as a "non-profit organization providing free visual and performing arts classes to children in Los Angeles." Sherry Jason and her husband, Bob, both former criminal defense attorneys, share the philosophy that art represents a powerful transformational tool in young people's lives. In 1984 they teamed to channel their efforts toward child and teenage rehabilitation; together they founded *City Hearts*, an organization using theatre methods to help children at risk. Twenty years later, they have been enjoying the fruits of their labors. During this period, *City Hearts*, through a wide variety of programs, has amply demonstrated its ability to lift the often-battered lives of teenage children to high levels of self-worth and hope.

According to Sherry, the impulse of the organization is both preventive and curative. The *City Hearts* Mission Statement reads as follows:

"City Hearts: Kids Say 'Yes' To The Arts" intervenes in a loving, supportive and nurturing way to break the cycle of poverty, neglect, abuse, homelessness, delinquency and violence that destroy children. Through the discipline and healing of arts education and performance experience, City Hearts provides positive role mod-

119

els, enrichment and inspiration for children to become productive, creative, law-abiding members of society."

A 1992 "Sentenced to the Stage" program devised by *City Hearts* offered young offenders the opportunity to work in theatre classes as an option to public service, and this program has produced certifiable results.

In February of 2003, Sherry granted me a telephone interview:

RM: What led you to abandon your successful work as a defense lawyer and take up this work?

SJ: I remember from the time I was little that I wanted to make the world a better place. This desire continued through the days when I was a defense lawyer. The children of City Hearts begin their young lives in despair. Through the magic of the arts, we lead them to inspiration and triumph.

RM: Was there any pivotal moment you can recall that led you to take up this work?

SJ: Yes. In 1977, as a new attorney, I toured Los Angeles Central Juvenile Hall where I watched in sadness and fascination as a convicted thirteen-year-old murderer took his first piano lesson. He was a prodigy, the music of Mozart touching his soul. I wondered what would have happened if he had met the piano before he met the gangs.

RM: How has your organization grown since those early days?

SJ: We now have a beautiful studio in downtown Los Angeles, and another site in Oxnard, north of L.A., in Ventura County, an area that is even worse than Tijuana (Mexico) for its deprived conditions and crime. We still take in about 500 schoolchildren a week at our home studio, and more are covered by the Oxnard branch which takes our teachers into the schools in after-school programs in dance, acting, poetry and playwriting.

RM: What other factors have moved you to carry on all these years?

SJ: A ripple effect was breaking the hearts of families. But many of these children were effectively thrown away by their own parents. What I saw was that these were really nice kids! I saw that we have to nurture and care for these children. We did one program in a 16-week facility (detention center) program. We saw rival kids become brothers. They said, "Now we have become brothers and now we can show people our hearts." A follow-up to this activity came from the facility superintendent who stated that all the boys participating in a full academic program wanted only to remain with the director and the theatre program. All else became secondary! They became model prisoners.

RM: What would you most like to see happen in the line of prison reform?

SJ: I'd like to see the base of the triangle which is currently the prison system—that is, incarceration, and the lobbyists for political action committees for the guards' unions—flipped around, and that the base becomes the nurturing enrichment programs for children."[*]

The successes with children of the *City Hearts* program has been liberally documented in both media and government circles. A long list of impressive educational and governmental organizations, including The President's Committee on the Arts and Humanities, the National Endowment for the Arts, and the United

*Telephone interview with the author, February 12, 2003.

States Department of Justice have conferred special citations on *City Hearts.*

City Hearts has sponsored an impressively diverse array of programs through the years. These have included:

1993: "From Gangs to the Stage," the City Hearts program serving incarcerated youth in Los Angeles County.

1994: The aforementioned "Sentenced to the Stage" initiative.

1994: "Youth Arts Diversion," targeting youth between ages 11–17, and "The Early Years" programs, ages 5–10 specifically designed to bring arts education to disadvantaged children living in high-crime communities.

1996: "For Girls Only" project launched with special workshops and classes.

1997: ALITE—"Arts and Literacy for Tomorrow's Education" teaching language and learning skills through playwriting, music, dance, circus and theatre arts. Included in this program is an involvement with the poetry, themes and characters of Shakespeare.

1999: City Hearts free Summer Camp of the Arts providing over 1000 children, ages 5–11, with daily arts classes.

1999: City Hearts Photography: "Fresh Focus: A New Shot at Life": Photography program begins for youth on probation in Van Nuys and downtown Los Angeles.

2009: City Hearts celebrates 25 years of service to the community.

The ambitious energy behind this broad array of programs, the self-sacrifice of Bob Jason, putting his entire retirement savings toward the construction of a dance floor, and the determination by the Jasons to make the project work at whatever cost, has brought inspiring moments of fruition. In an article entitled "Grassroots," printed in the January-February, 1997 edition of the magazine, *Living Fit*, Sherry Jason states:

> ". . . I've seen the lives of kids really change. A case in point is a young Hispanic man we'll call Mike. When he came to the program, Mike was a 17-year-old gang member with a drug-addicted mother and a life going nowhere. Now, at 20, he is entering the University of California at Los Angeles, where he will major in accounting."

Sherry adds:

> "We're hoping he'll come back after graduation and do bookkeeping and data analysis for us!"[*]

Gus Rogerson and the 52nd Street Project
(DVD disc 1: section 6)

The possibilities of our kids when given a safe place

"Time and time again the kids keep coming back. They don't want to leave."

—Director Gus Rogerson

Three thousand miles away from *City Hearts*, but sharing a similar intention, is New York City's *52nd Street Project*. This organization is also dedicated to taking children and teenagers from

*Ibid.

the harshness of the city streets and giving them a "safe place" where their talents can blossom.

Gus Rogerson is the artistic director of New York City's *52nd Street Project*, where young people from New York City's Hell's Kitchen neighborhood, a region which extends roughly from 42nd to 59th Streets south to north, and from 8th to 12th Avenues east to west, find their way to the doors of the Project. They are not limited to this area, but may come from any of the five boroughs of New York City. Once at the Project, they gather for theatre classes, rehearsals and the presentation of live performances on a wide variety of themes.

Director Rogerson works in partnership with Executive Director Carol Ochs and an additional staff of four full-time and four part-time workers. Rogerson started volunteering in 1992 and joined the staff in 1998, replacing founder Willy Reale as Artistic Director. He now also functions as actor, director, mentor and writer. The original objective of the group, according to Rogerson, was to bring children from the tough Hell's Kitchen neighborhood together with professional artists to create original theatre. A substantial part of the work is now accomplished when these young people are taken from the streets and brought into a revitalizing contact with nature where they work under the supervision of theatre professionals in creating original plays. Director Rogerson describes the activity of the theatre:

> *Basically we use writing and performing of plays as a way of raising self-esteem, giving kids the experience of success. They find us, and we are currently working with a hundred a year.*
>
> *The first program, called "Playmaking," runs for eight weeks, and introduces 10 and 11-year-old children to playwriting.*
>
> *We avoid selection, and anytime a kid participates in a program, whether they're acting or writing, they are the star. It's ten kids. They learn about playwriting. At the end of that process, they are introduced to professional actors and an adult director, known as a "dramaturg" (an expert in dramatic writing). The kid who is*

about to write the play interviews the actors. We go away to the country for the weekend and under the helpful guidance of the dramaturg, the kid writes the play. That play is subsequently produced in New York. Theatre professionals present it where we can find space. On that weekend we give four performances, and when the play is performed, the child playwright is sitting on stage watching at a desk. The founder of this concept was Daniel Judah Sklar, who wrote the book, Playmaking, *and Willie Reale, who devised a manual called* 52 Pick-Up.

Rogerson adds with a note of delight:

"Time and time again the kids keep coming back. They don't want to leave. They find us, and they just keep coming through the door."[*]

On a winter night in 2000, I attended a show at the *52nd Street Project's* studio, consisting of original scenes conceived and written by its young directors and featuring actors from the group interacting with their mentors. There was a lively interchange, and afterwards a spirited post-show discussion which included a full house of supporters. An infectious enthusiasm filled the little theatre, and one could sense the budding feelings of authority and pride in the young playwrights.

The creative and socializing mission of *The 52nd Street Project* was well on track.

---

*Telephone interview with Gus Rogerson, October 3, 1999.

David Booth

On being subversive.

"I have to know the enemy, know how it works, be able to defend myself and then do what I want."[*]

On October 19, 1998, I arrived at the office of David Booth at the Ontario Institute of Secondary Education (OISE) at a happy moment. As Professor of Arts, Dr. Booth had just been honored for twenty-five years of prestigious service by OISE as drama teacher, consultant and theatre educator. Dr. Booth's distinguished career has focused mainly on the development of what is known as story theatre, and his widely read book, *Story Drama: Reading, writing and role-playing across the curriculum*, is considered a classic by theatre educators. *Story Drama* involves a method that encourages young students to act out events based on their own lives, where real and fictional elements may be merged in releasing buried feelings.

In *Story Drama*, Booth acknowledges the debt he owes to a "community of teachers working with freedom and generosity."

It has been the inspiration and example of these associates, in addition to my own initial willingness to plunge in during those early days when my basic problem was survival.[**]

Booth expands this indebtedness to include many young students:

*David Booth, interview with author, April 23, 1997.
**Booth, *Story Drama*, 9.

126

And what those children did non-verbally with their bodies thrilled me to my core and I suddenly recognized the power of letting the drama emerge from the children's imaginations as opposed to my giving them constant instructions and orders. . . .[*]

Booth describes the methodology of his approach in drawing out the spontaneity of the child.

Students can plumb stories which originate from such diverse sources as "personal anecdotes, folk tales, novels and picture books." Thus nothing is out of bounds to the imaginative process of the child in the course of creation. The role of the teacher in the classroom is also a fluid and lively possibility. The teacher can play a shaping role which can suggest, guide and help to inspire the vision of the story, but not dominate the process of the child's creative process. Techniques are also wide open. They may include any number of created stories in which one might find "choral reading, movement, dance drama, storytelling, writing in role, teacher in role.[**]

Booth further recounts the methods and effects of group collaboration.

Will I know which road to follow with each group? This is the drama teacher's struggle—listening, watching, setting up situations that will foreshadow the direction of the journey, knowing when to intervene, when to use a particular strategy to open up discussion, to move the children into action, to cause them to pause, to reflect, to rethink and all this without predetermining the learning, the content, the meat of the lesson. We provide the plasticene for them to model, and in drama, we will sculpt together, each move affecting all others, the individual finding

*Ibid., 11.
**Ibid., 63.

strength from the group, and the group enriching and extending to each individual. I'm afraid I spend little time in "one-on-one" in drama teaching, for having sensed the power of the group, I want to unleash it so that children can together create a play that, perhaps without audience, will reveal the thrill of theatre, of using improvised dialogue to build our sense of story. They will know when we have completed our work, and they will recognize the aesthetic power of theatrical collaboration.[*]

Like many other TIE educators, Booth is aware that the theatre educator must work within a system which, more often than not, fails to appreciate the significance of theatre as a learning tool. He spoke to me about these issues:

RM: Would you discuss the status of the theatre-in-education movement today, particularly in its relationship with the current academic establishment?

DB: You see this institution OISE (Ontario Institute of Secondary Education) is a counter-culture institution born in the 60's, mainly American. It was a white ivory tower which had holes in it challenging education. Now we train teachers here, so we have to follow the dictates of the government more strongly, and this year we're being inspected by the government and accredited, and if we don't get the accreditation, well . . . you can hear it under my voice, can't you?

RM: Yes.

DB: Within that, I'm still as creative as I want to be. But within that I have to know the enemy, know how it works, be able to de-

*Ibid., 51.

fend myself and then do what I want—with an added burden now that I didn't have in the 60's.

RM: You have to become a subversive?

DB: Absolutely. That was Neil Postman's term (referring to the late Neil Postman's book, Teaching as a Subversive Activity). And to be subversive you have to know the legal part. You see you can't just be subversive.

RM: You just can't . . .

DB: That's right, you get fired! Now the question is, is it worth being subversive to maintain your goal? Because it always has been that way. It's just that it's more formalized and ritualized now. But it's harder because those rituals now are very, very defined and articulated. So you can't just fluff them off like I did in the 70's. You have to meet them, explain them, and get on with your work.

RM: You have to demystify what you're doing in the face of institutional skepticism and opposition?

DB: That's right. We're in the demystification process at the moment. That doesn't mean that we have to lose our mythology. It means we have to "de-myth" it for the public.[*]

Story Drama is a valued volume with educators, and seems destined to remain so.

*David Booth in Toronto, Ontario, interview with author, April 23, 1997.

Lee Willingham

The multiple intelligences conferred by music

*"I've seen athletes write in their reflective journals to me, 'If I did-
n't have music class, I don't know how I would survive my day.' "*
—Dr. Lee Willingham

Lee Willingham, Professor of Music Education at the University of Toronto, considers himself a disciple of David Booth.
Though music and theatre may identify two different approaches
to learning, Willingham makes far-reaching connections between
the two with his students. He is equally eloquent in describing the
potential of the arts in education.

As Willingham conducts a class with a group of future teaching candidates preparing to work in the Ontario school system, an
exciting ring of enthusiasm fills the classroom. "Holistic is what
we are!" he proclaims.

In one session, the class of some twenty-odd students was invited to record the sounds of everyday life as the basis for an improvised musical piece. Silence was called for, and at the end of a
minute, the students were asked to recall what sounds they had
heard. A hissing radiator, the drone of a subway, and a slamming
door were recorded. The class was then transformed into a
three-part orchestra consisting of "hissers," "droners" and "slam-
mers." Assuming the role of conductor, Willingham proceeded to
shape these sounds into an environmentally-inspired symphonic
movement. The contagious joy of making music was apparent to
all, a quality that Willingham hopes will continue to fill future
classrooms of the Canadian public schools.

Later, students were urged to use their bodies in moving through
various musical selections. Each of four groups was to agree upon a
movement pattern to illustrate a children's song, "Boom, Boom,

Ain't it Great to be Crazy?" Here body and mind coalesced in an exuberant performance. I recalled thinking, "The awakening of a happy family of jolly gnomes on Christmas morning."

Lee Willingham, who is also a highly respected choir director in Toronto, granted me an interview at his OISE building office:

RM: Will you speak of the effects of music on your students?

LW: I have some general observations. I think that the arts provide a really unique experience in a school setting that is industrially based. So the arts provide students with a whole other environment that isn't so concerned with the economic outcomes. And so when kids, who we see at risk, when we see them engaged in making music or painting or dancing, we see another spiritual dimension come out in them. And I can tell you that as a coordinator of music in a large inner city school board, I saw kids that would be robbing milk stores, planning to steal drugs for a few hours after school, completely focused, completely into it, understanding their responsibility to the troupe and the ensemble. I've seen athletes whom I thought were gifted athletes but marginally gifted musically, write in their reflective journals to me, "If I didn't have music class, I don't know how I would survive my day." . . . The thing that I noticed overall is that—well, one of my superintendents used to say that the arts "tenderize us" . . . "humanize us."

RM: Are there any classroom experiences that stand out to you?

LW: This brilliant violinist is in my class. We got violins for everybody, and he walked us through two hours of violin playing. At the end, we did a little quiz on the multiple intelligences, or Howard Gardner's "seven ways of knowing."

RM: He mentions, if I remember, seven ways we can be intelligent.

LW: That's right. There's linguistic, there's musical, there's logical, there's visual, spatial, there's kinesthetic—some people know best by moving—there's the inter-personal—some people know best by socializing—and there's the intra-personal, and I asked,

"What were we working on today when we were working on this musical thing? What different ways of knowing? It's not how smart are you? but 'How are you smart?' How are we smart in this class today?" Well, we decided that we were linguistic, of course. We talked about it; we were visual—we looked at the instrument, we visualized it, we conceptualized it—a three-dimensional thing. It was kinesthetic—we had to do all kinds of motor muscle things; it was logical—there's nothing more logical than a violin, its patterns, its sequences. It's mathematical—it's tuned in fifths; it's certainly musical—that's a given. It was intra-personal—we interacted with each other, we socialized, we had to actually. I had to see what you were doing—I was checking myself. And it was reflective—because we all had to think about our insights. . . . So just in doing one little task in a musical environment, our whole being was being engaged in this rich experience!

RM: You might say that in this exercise of learning violin playing, the students were growing in related "intelligences."

LW: Exactly!! It made me think about brain-based research and how that neurons fire in connection with the synapses in the brain, and certain activities strengthen the synaptic connections. So that neuron firing is truer and stronger. Literally, when we were learning to play the violin, we were growing brains. In our classroom today we were growing brains! We were deepening the synaptic connections in the brain that enabled us, as they became stronger and bolder and richer, to become more knowing, aware, and confident about what we do.

And that to me is what the arts do for kids! It's this whole thing. You can't say, "Well, the arts build self-esteem." Of course they do. But you could get self-esteem anywhere. But I'd like to commend the arts for much deeper, much wider things that happen with us. [*]

*David Willingham, interview with the author, October 1998.

Sunna Rasch and the Periwinkle National Theatre
(DVD disc 1: section 8)

Self-knowledge leading to vital transformations

"The play you gave made me see what I was doing. Thank you for sharing the play with me. It made me think."
>—A fourteen-year-old abandoned child, after seeing a 1988 *Periwinkle National Theatre* performance of *Halfway There*

Sunna Rasch, director and founder of *The Periwinkle National Theater* since 1963 and now the oldest non-profit children's theatre in America, conceives of Periwinkle as an instrument for social change.

The *Periwinkle* production, "Halfway There" is a play about five teenagers who come to terms with their feelings about drug addiction. It neither preaches nor lectures, but rather allows the five young actors from multi-cultural backgrounds a free voice in confronting the addictive habits which had at one time poisoned their lives. Sunna Rasch discussed the motivating forces that led to the formation of her theatre.

From the first, I wanted to move the children to a feeling basis. I wanted them to reflect on their behavior, and to understand issues emotionally as a means of change. Now there is no doubt that this is working and touching their lives. A lady who saw "Halfway There" in New Jersey came to my door to talk. She said that one half of the kids that saw the show came immediately to talk with a drug counselor or to thank Periwinkle for giving them the courage to stand up to peer pressure.[*]

*Sunna Rasch interview, New York, June 11, 1997.

133

Presenting productions on a wide range of contemporary social issues, *The Periwinkle National Theatre* has played to audiences of over five million, nationally and internationally. Its style has been eclectic, freely embracing various forms of poetry, music and dance. Audiences have ranged from elementary grade students to those in high school and college.

Periwinkle has attracted extensive official recognition for their work. In May, 2000, they received national awards from The Executive Office of the President, adding to citations from The Office of National Drug Control Policy, The John Stanford Educational Heroes Award and the U.S. Department of Education. In June of 2000, *Periwinkle* was awarded the prestigious annual Sara Spenser Award for Meritorious Contribution to Children's Theatre, presented by the American Alliance for Theatre and Education in Washington, D.C.

Sunna Rasch suggested some factors which led to her work:

With the changing conditions of our society urged by the decay of the family, and the consequent descent into hopelessness which characterizes our children today, I am even more convinced of the need for a theatre which can penetrate to the soul of the child and lead this child to hope and to feeling a sense of his or her own potential. There is no doubt that we are doing this. [*]

The effectiveness of the production, "Halfway There," has been confirmed in letters from many children. Here is one example:

"To the cast: My name is—. I am 14 years old. I am living in a

*Ibid.

group home. The reason I am in here is because of drugs and steal-ing. The play that you gave, made me see what I was doing. As your play showed that kids were stealing and using drugs and then get-ting sent away. This is exactly what happened to me. . . . I haven't seen my parents since I got to this place and it's been about three months. I miss them a lot. Thank you for sharing the play with me. It made me think. . . . Thank you."

Most of the *Periwinkle* productions for school ages have a strong social agenda. "Split Decision" confronts the problems of divorce and single parent homes; "Rooftop," of bullying in our schools today; "Little Red Riding Hood Finds the Safety Zone!" of abduction prevention for very young children. Their latest pro-duction, "The Birthday Party that Almost Wasn't" features a young boy who learns, in the words of Rasch, "Manners, apprecia-tion and respect for others."

Sunna Rasch explains her company's odyssey in terms of a relentless quest to reach as many children as possible. This has been accompanied by an equally dedicated effort to attract finan-cial support. Says Rasch:

Somehow it has appeared! We touch lives. We have to be humble about it. But you become so impassioned. It's like—and I hate to use this word—but it's like an addiction! I haven't had a vacation in ten years."

She sighs. But before the sigh can admit a note of defeat, the eyes of Sunna Rasch twinkle and she adds, "Maybe someday!"

Alli Chagi-Starr
(DVD disc 1: section 9)

Theatre: changing the world through peaceful means

"There was something in that moment where I learned that what we had was the anti-weapon. That we have art. That we have the power to disarm."

—Alli Chagi-Starr

The TIE movement, since its inception in the mid-seventies, was identified as a tool for social change. Issues such as monopoly, greed in high places, clean air and toxic waste dominated its concerns even in those days. This focus on social issues brought the movement into sharp confrontation with government policy makers.

This factor of reform continues today. Perhaps the most noted figure of our times to utilize theatre to urge social change is the Brazilian theatre innovator, Augusto Boal. In the mid-1970's Boal marched giant masks through the streets of San Paolo to challenge the killing of orphaned street children. These and other issues protesting governmental policies, led to his imprisonment on three occasions, but never defeated his purposes. Boal is currently an official in the Brazilian government. He is also a world-renowned teacher, and his methods developed toward liberating the oppressed members of society are described in his books, *Theatre of the Oppressed* and *Rainbow of Desire.*

The American artist Peter Schumann is an heir to Boal. Schumann has specialized in the creation and use of giant puppets originating from his workshop in Glover, Vermont, in protesting a wide range of official policies. One dramatization was a visceral protest of the Vietnam War; more current examples have included official practices of trade organizations and banks which trample the rights of the poorer classes in our society. In St. Louis in the 1990's I witnessed a protest of the practices of the World Bank and its victimization of the poor classes of underdeveloped nations.[*]

The tradition of theatre as social protest continues, and one of its highly active practitioners is Alli Chagi-Starr, who utilizes dance and other movement-based techniques to seek justice for the oppressed. Chagi-Starr has been active since 1991 and is currently the Art and Media Director for *Reclaim the Future* at the Ella Baker Center for Human Rights in Oakland, California. She has led groups such as *Art in Action Youth Leadership Program* and *Dancers without Borders.*

Chagi-Starr has guided thousands to employ non-violent methods through creative means, but, along with many other demonstrating artists, has had to face police opposition. She appeared on May 12, 2006 on the Principia College campus where she lectured on her work, and then provided a lively workshop on non-violent protest techniques for a large group of students. In an interview following her presentation, I asked her some questions:

RM: First, could you tell us what led you to this work that you are doing?

AC: I was in a pickup truck in 1995 and traveling across the country to educate people about Muma Abu Jamal who is a political prisoner—who was framed for killing a police officer in the 80's and is now over 25 years on death row in Pennsylvania. I wanted to use art to get the word out about his case and what had happened. . . . He had been speaking out about the bombing of the MOVE ORGANIZATION which was an alternative black organization in

*Vivid pictorial coverage of these events may be found in the Ronald T. Simon and Marc Estrin book, *Rehearsing with Gods: Photographs and Essays on the Bread and Puppet Theatre.*

Philadelphia which would not be suppressed. They were exposing the violence that was being perpetrated on their communities.

RM: Was this the key incident in turning you toward this work?

AC: This was one of the key incidents. This was a turning point anyway. My mom had been an activist when I was growing up and I was inspired by her work. Also my father is a deeply ethical, charismatic man—not political per se but the type of person who would return a dollar if someone undercharged him. So we traveled around the country in a pickup truck for 7 ½ months and I did a lot of education around Muma Abu Jamal, for anyone who cared to listen. I gathered groups together and we created theatre. We created jails out of cardboard, and we tore them apart in the middle of the street and freed Jamal's image. A lot of communities asked us if we would burn an image of this judge that had sentenced Muma. Many felt it was a very racist sentencing, but we said that we would not burn an effigy, there was already too much imagery of violence and destruction. We know what that looks like. But we wanted to ask, "What does liberation look like?" "What does liberation feel like and how can we show that through art?" So that was the major work traveling around the country for 7 ½ months in 1995.

RM: And how did that lead to the other aspects of your career?

AC: I came from a very intense technical dance background. I studied all different techniques, Limon, Cunningham and ballet, and so I had always wanted to figure out what was the bridge between dance and particularly technical dance that I had grown up learning, and activism. But there was something missing. I wanted to find a way to bridge dance and activism. I found that trying to get dancers, trained dancers, to do activism was much harder than working with activists who were willing to dance. (Laugh)

RM: What did this transition from dance to activism entail?

138

AC: What did that look like? Well, what it entailed for me was coming back to the Bay area and starting different dance companies and mostly doing a lot of street theatre so we would be invited by other organizations or labor unions or church groups to do a theatre piece about a particular issue. I started a dance group with some friends called The Emma Said Dance Company, and Emma, after Emma Goldman, who said, "If I can't dance, I don't want to join your revolution!" or something to that effect! (Laugh) And so it's now called "Emma Said Dance Theatre."

RM: What happened there?

AC: We went up to Seattle during the WTO (World Trade Organization) protest—we actually helped mobilize for it—in a dance theatre road show where we mobilized probably somewhere between five and ten thousand people to come to Seattle. We not only inspired them through theatre to come and learn about what the World Trade Organization was doing to the rest of the planet and the people of the planet, but we trained people in non-violence and civil disobedience and dance theatre and puppet-making, and how to talk to media about the issues surrounding the WTO so that when they came to Seattle, they were trained in all of these techniques.

RM: How did the techniques of non-violence play out in Seattle?

AC: Well, what we saw in Seattle was fifty to eighty thousand people participating in non-violent direct action through the arts, and with the technique of "each one teach one" it spread like wildfire. And all of a sudden there was this chant (singing and clapping rhythmically) "This is what democracy looks like!" all through the streets. . . . It was so inspiring, and then there was this real crescendo on that day of Tuesday, November 20th, 1999. We had been in the rain since four or five in the morning. We'd been holding down the street, and we really had to decide for ourselves, this couldn't just be your average everyday march, it really had to be

139

"We really can't let this meeting happen. We're sorry, but when these men get together and meet, people die, and our planet is threatened, and devastated. And we just cannot, in good faith, allow this meeting to go on." And thousands of us came to that conclusion—that we had to shut the meeting down.

RM: *Were there challenging moments with the police?*

AC: *Oh, yes. There was a moment when people had been pepper-sprayed and tear-gassed. The police had never seen anything this impactful and effective. And the police were holding strong beautiful young people who were locked down and held in u-locks by the necks and the people who had been pepper-sprayed all day but they were still smiling through their tears and through the fear that they were living through that day. . . . There was this one intersection—you have to imagine intersections all across downtown Seattle filled with people—but this one it looked—this tense moment—it looked like this, like these flanks of cops moving in and they were at this platform where these young people—about twenty of them—were locked down. We started to sing, and one of my friends, Julie, started singing "Amazing Grace" and all of a sudden there were hundreds of people singing whatever words they knew of that melody.*

RM: *It sounds like an American Tiannemen Square.*

AC: *I wasn't in Tiannemen, but I felt what those courageous people at Tiannemen, must have felt, some of them killed for their beliefs.*

RM: *Were there any casualties with all that violence?*

AC: *Well, none of us died that day. But many of us with white-skin privilege don't realize the risks our brothers and sisters of color face when they stand up for their rights. We were blessed. But we sang the song and the police backed off from the march and from the protest. . . . There was something in that moment where I*

140

learned that what we had was the anti-weapon. That we have art. That we have the power to disarm. We change things through the power of community and art.

RM: Are there images that come back to you when you think about that day?

AC: I remember this moment with my hands reaching up to the sky looking through my fingers and I could see the tear gas and the fog. But the sun was trying to come out and there were glints of light coming through all the women and their hands in the air and the music all around. <u>And the police lowered their weapons! And I just knew that day was ours! . . . And I knew it was possible with art.</u>[*]

*Alli Chagi-Starr, interview with the author, May 11, 2006.

EIGHT

BUILDING BRIDGES TO THE COMMUNITY

I must study politics and war that my sons may have liberty to study mathematics and philosophy. My sons ought to study, geography, natural history, naval architecture, navigation, commerce, and agriculture, in order to give their children a right to study painting, poetry, music, architecture, statuary, tapestry and porcelain.

—John Adams on "Priorities," in a Letter to Abigail Adams,
May 12, 1780

"Whatever the reason, it is evident that for most anti-theatrical polemicists, playgoing tends to rank abnormally high in the hierarchy of sins," writes Jonas Barish in *The Anti-theatrical Prejudice.*[*] This book details the wide range of social attitudes that have served to denigrate theatre through history. We may be surprised to learn that anti-theatre bias has been advanced from cultural figures such as Plato, Rousseau, Diderot, Samuel Johnson and Charles Lamb. Theatre educators should be aware of these attitudes which may still linger in the minds of school boards today.

Much of ancient prejudice against theatre centered around change. This was rooted in the Puritan's belief that a man should

---

*Barish, *The Anti-theatrical Prejudice*, 80.

142

not stray from his given nature, the concept of Man created in the image and likeness of God. In transforming himself before the public, the actor affirms this transgression. Thus, according to Barish:

Men come closest to God when they preserve themselves as unchanging as possible, when they yield as little as they can to their natural bent for mutability.[*]

Change, or the presenting of multiple appearances, was often looked upon as the devil's tool which could only spread confusion. Barish cites Machiavelli's *The Prince:*

Chapter 18 of The Prince notoriously advises the ruler to combine the strength of the lion with the cunning of the fox; to disguise, moreover, the fox's slyness with the appearance of innocence. It helps to be "a great feigner and dissembler"; and men are so simple and so ready to obey present necessities, that one who deceives will always find those who allow themselves to be deceived.

Anti-theatrical prejudice emanated from many other sources. Charles Lamb declared that plays were better when read, and that the effects of lighting, sound, and makeup imposed a barrier to reflection. Observing dramatic action spoiled one's peace of mind and tranquility.

Author Barish sums up many other areas of prejudice:

In Rousseau's eyes, the actor's trade corrupts him, alienating him from his true self. Diderot reverses the order; for him, the actor lacks a self to begin with, and it is because he has no character of his own that he is able to assume so many imaginary ones. In their offstage lives, he finds them repellent: "Polite, caustic, and cold.

*Ibid., 105.

Ostentatious, dissipated, wasteful, self interested . . . isolated, vagabond, at the back of the great; few morals, no friends, almost none of those sweet and holy ties which bind us to the pains and pleasures of another, who in turn shares our own." Why do they go onto the stage in the first place? "Lack of education, poverty, a libertine spirit. The stage is a resource, never a choice. No-one ever became an actor out of love or virtue, from desire to be useful in the world, or to serve his country and family; or from any of the honorable motives which might lead a right mind, a warm heart, a sensitive soul, to so fine a profession."[*]

Well! And Barish offers a dim view in ending anti-theatrical prejudice.

. . . the persistence of the struggle seems to suggest that it is more than a temporary skirmish: it reflects an abiding tension in our natures as social beings. On the one hand we wish to license the fullest mimetic exploration of our condition—for self-understanding, delight, and self-mastery. But to do so through the medium of other human beings like ourselves means licensing the liberation of much that we wish ultimately to control. . . . So long as we seek to render the quality of our existence in voice, gesture, and color, the simple integrity to which we all at heart aspire will continue to haunt us. To this integrity the antitheatrical prejudice will continue to pay its wry tribute, preserving our awareness of the corruption we risk in the very act of attempting to express and subdue it.[**]

This dim view of ending society's historical prejudices against the stage could, taken literally, seem to provide a Sisyphean task to the theatre educator proposing a new program. But

*Ibid., 281.
**The Prince and the Discourses, ed. Max Lerner. Trans. Luigi Ricci and E.R.P. Vincent Modern Library, New York, 1950.

we must show ourselves adept in dispelling such prejudices with authoritative logic.

Let's take the subject of "change," for example, that a prospective school superintendent may fear. "I wonder if this drama person may be out to change my school," he may be thinking. At an interview we should be prepared to answer this fear even before it is voiced.

"*Tell us what you want to learn, and we will help you to learn it,*" TIE authority, Scott Miller of the Children's Theatre of Charlotte, North Carolina, declared at the 1997 Washington, D.C. conference of The Alliance for Theatre in Higher Education. Miller is recommending here that the TIE teacher's role lies not in *altering* what is being taught, but in *supporting* it. "*If you want history taught better, this is how. Or if math, here's how we produce better mathematicians,*" emphasized Miller. This kind of thinking immediately identifies the educator as a supporter of the faculty.

Miller continued with the mention of another theme, that of demystification:

> "*We must demystify what we do to help teach what they are already teaching. We must then find the process that fits in with theirs. It comes down to discovering 'what are the needs of the school?'*"

The process of building bridges between the school and the TIE instructor involves advocacy, or the process of speaking up for the use of arts in education. Many theatre educators are not, for one reason or another, sufficiently equipped to demonstrate the enormous potential of an arts program. Bryar Cougle, Arts Education Consultant at the North Carolina Department of Public Instruction spoke on this issue at the same conference.

> *We can talk about all these things (what arts can do for kids) but until we let the world know that we're doing these things and until the world respects that we're doing these things, we probably*

aren't going to get very far in selling the arts as a primary part of every child's education. . . . I am convinced that the teachers, the arts teachers in the schools could take education back for themselves. I think they have to do it and they have to do it at the classroom level. But they have to get really smart and savvy. They have to know what they're doing, they have to identify it.

Advocacy is a kind of "selling job," if you like, but one which all educators must be prepared to take on if theatre is to advance to center stage in the classroom. It comes down to sharing authentic and documented information with enthusiasm. This enthusiasm must be founded both upon what we can document, and also what we deeply know and believe about the effectiveness of theatre in an educational program. This requires a good bit of preparation. A "pitch" for a theatre program, cannot substitute for a program's efficacy—in the same way that a smartly fashioned brochure for a new Toyota can never substitute for a good drive—but it can serve to open the front door and get the superintendent into a front seat whereby he can view the landscape.

Here are the kinds of things that an educator should be able to share with the superintendent or school board in proposing a program:

Why the arts, and specifically theatre, are important in education. There is much available documentation readily obtainable from such organizations as the (American) National Endowment for the Arts, The President's Council, and books such as *Learning the Arts in an Age of Uncertainty* by Walter Pitman, and James Moffett's *The Universal Schoolhouse.* There is so much authoritative material on a philosophical level on what the arts can achieve for our students, in writings ranging from Plato to Dewey to Herbert Read, whom Moffett cites in his *The Universal Schoolhouse*:

. . . Herbert Read agreed with Dewey that art is a universal language that breaks down national and ethnic barriers. . . . The fact that the arts are serious modes of knowing in the highest forms of

146

play explains why someone like Read would advocate them as the basics of learning—the thesis of his Education Through Art. [*]

How theatre is helping our young people academically. The following is part of the comprehensive 1998 Stanford University-based Shirley Brice Heath report, compiled over a period of ten years, and cited in the November 13th issue of *The San Francisco Chronicle* that year:

A Stanford University professor has found that youngsters who dance, act, sing and paint in [after–school] programs are more likely to win academic awards and achieve, yet most American students have no weekly arts education.

"It doesn't mean that if your child paints a picture, he or she automatically will achieve academically," said the author of the research, Shirley Brice Heath. The Stanford professor of English and linguistics is also a senior scholar at the Carnegie Foundation for the Advancement of Teaching.

The research, however, demonstrates that children in the arts use linguistic and cognitive thinking skills—such as long-term planning, critiquing and focused attention that can reap positive social and academic benefits. Heath's findings, presented in Oakland at a meeting of the East Bay Community Foundation, come at a time when most students in California and the rest of the country have no weekly arts education during school hours.

According to the study, young people who work in the arts are:

- *Four times more likely to win an academic award, such as being named to the honor roll.*

- *Eight times more likely to win a community service award.*

- *Three times more likely to win a school attendance award.*

*Moffett, *Schoolhouse*, 77.

- *Four times more likely to participate in a math or science fair.*

The young people in these arts programs engage in lots of communication similar to the kind you would find in a venture capital company when everyone is sitting around the boardroom talking about the kind of project they "want to develop," said Heath. "Or in a software company."

The ten-year national study was based on records of 30,000 young people participating in programs run by 124 youth organizations in 30 locations from Massachusetts to Hawaii. The children in the study were from predominantly urban areas and they were more likely than the average youngster to be on welfare or from a divorced family.

The findings add to a growing body of work that links achievement and other positive behavior to arts education.

For example, a study of 1995 SAT college admission test scores found that students who had studied the arts for more than four years scored higher than students who did not. The scores were 59 points higher on the verbal section and 44 points higher in math.[*]

Get a sense of what is going on at the school. Is there a lack of enthusiasm for studies? Is crime a problem? Theft? Drugs? Segregation? Bullying? You should be prepared to show how theatre has helped with all these issues in producing an ensemble spirit; care for one's neighbor; enthusiasm and real engagement in learning; harmonizing relationships between students, faculty and staff; elevating the level of morale; reducing absenteeism and dropouts; and in reducing delinquency and crime. There are many publications testifying to the efficacy of theatre in these issues, such that published by the President's Commission, *Coming Up*

* "Study Links Art Classes to Academic Achievement," *San Francisco Chronicle*. November 13, 1998. (A 22)

Taller: Arts and Humanities Programs for Children and Youth at Risk.* Statements such as the following written by educator Hughes Mearns might be useful.

> *All the arts combine in the theatre, décor, the dance imperson-ation, effective speech, the song, pantomime and the projection of personality, the art of suppressing self, and even ill will, for the sake of unity of effort. Hundreds of other arts could be listed in-cluding the art of living together and the art of creative imagina-tion. That is why the play can never be omitted from child education.***

In harmonizing the school atmosphere, there is one factor that is hardly ever discussed in conferences advocating a theatre program; the involvement with beauty. According to leading theo-rists, the cultivation of an aesthetic sense in the experience of a young person will have lasting effects on character throughout a lifetime. Plato, Santayana, Alfred North Whitehead, George Ber-nard Shaw, and Herbert Read all affirm this connection.

Read, writing in the early and mid-20th Century, was one of the most perceptive social critics in our times to make the connec-tion between the activity of art and its subsequent effects on char-acter. In his book, *The Hell With Culture,* he states:

> *Finally, I must mention this argument for aesthetic education which Plato regarded as the most important of all—the moral ar-gument. The same idea is implicit in Schiller, in Hebart, in Nietzche, and even in Rousseau and Pestalozzi—even in Pav-lov!—the idea that a causal connection exists between action and character, between physical form and ethical form, between envi-ronment and virtue. Bring up your children, therefore in automatic obedience to the laws of aesthetic harmony, and you will naturally,*

*Weitz, *Coming Up Taller.*
**Mearns, *Creative Power,* 92.

149

inevitably, create in them a harmonious state of mind and feeling. [*]

Elsewhere Read analyzes the causes of violence and war as emanating from an enormous void in the lives of our citizens, or as he calls it,

a horror vacui: a fear of being alone, of having nothing to do, a neurosis whose symptoms are restlessness, and unmotivated and undirected rage, sinking at times into vapid listlessness. . . . This universal neurosis has developed step by step with the technological development of our civilization. It is the neurosis of men whose sole expenditure of energy is to pull a lever, or push a button, of men who have ceased to make things with their hands, even to transport themselves with their legs. [**]

The March 9, 2001 edition of *The New York Times* carries a photo of a group of young people taken at the time of the Santee massacre where two students were killed and thirteen injured. These teenagers are shown sprawled about on large rocks on the outskirts of town, doing nothing in particular. The scene is reminiscent of what we might see in any small town in America today at our shopping malls or on the stoops of our big cities, groups of teenagers just "hanging out." These scenes revealing kids companioning together, harmless in themselves, can be interpreted in another way: our kids have been given too little to do. There is a vacuum, as observed by Read, that needs to be filled. Art fills that void by providing our children with an activity that makes demands on them.

The current absorption with computers and video games fails to do this. We hear from sociologists and other social observers

*Read, Herbert. 1964. (373)
**Ibid., 378.

how this activity only creates "loners," and "egoists." Defenders of the video games claim that they build "hand-eye" coordination. But what about "*people*-coordination?" Precious little of that.

As for the effects of computers: According to separate commentators, they are hardly bringing us together, as some claim. Author, poet and social observer, Robert Bly writes:

The computer culture, an ineradicable element of sibling life, is producing isolation. ... The punished son exiled "to his own room," is now replaced by the Internet son. Computers, as we know, lead to a further drying up of conversation with adults, and the son becomes locked away from his own feelings. The ritual teacher Maring Prechtel believes that computer use is damaging young people more deeply than we understand. Young men have expressed their distance by putting on a hard computer shell, a kind of mechanical skin; but many young men now, modeling themselves—unconsciously—on computers, tend to be machine-like on the inside. They experience input and output. There's a loss of expressiveness and affiliation. [*]

For this reason, it was reassuring to watch a November 1st, 2007 television interview on the *Charlie Rose Show*. In this segment, Presidential Candidate Mike Huckabee was fervently pleading the case for the arts in education as his number one priority in education.

Huckabee: *Curriculum is too limited. If you want to succeed in education, you have a curriculum that touches* the talent of every child. *A good thing that's happened is that we put this new focus on math and science, and that's wonderful because kids need that and they have to be really challenged in it. But you know why nearly 6000 kids drop out of school every day in this country? ...* just think about that, 6,000—a third of the kids are going to drop out and never finish. *Why?* Because they're not dumb, they're just

*Bly, *The Sibling Society*, 128.

<u>bored.</u> *I suggest that we launch weapons of mass instruction in our music and arts programs. It's to touch the right brain as much as we're trying to touch the left brain. We have an education that is so tilted to left brain focus that we have forgotten that every human being has to have a balance of left and right side, the creative side and the logical side.*

Charlie Rose: *Tell me about the quality of teachers and how you think that that is a part of both the problem and the solution in America.*

Huckabee: *You don't encourage the kind of professionalism when you essentially treat teachers like factory workers in an assembly line. Teachers ought to be treated as professionals. They have professional degrees, they have professional backgrounds. And then we put them in a class and we say everybody gets the same pay.*

When asked by Rose what steps he would take to reform education in America:

Huckabee: *First, I'd put a big emphasis on music and art programs, the creative side, the right brain side. Secondly, I would make sure that we start focusing on the individual student . . . personalize education for the students. Third thing: I'd elevate and raise the prestige and level of teaching as a profession, and I'd encourage that we elevate both in terms of the stature we afford to them and in support. But also that we make it tangible that teachers actually get paid a professional level of salary and that when people go to college, they don't just say, "Well, I'd like to be a doctor or a nurse, I'd like to be a teacher, but I can't afford it because it doesn't pay enough, and I'll never pay off my college loan. . . ." The best creative teachers might get tossed because they're not necessarily robots, they're contrarians.* <u>But the contrarians make the best teachers.</u>[*]

*Excerpt from Charlie Rose—Mike Huckabee interview on the Public Television *Charlie Rose Show,* November 1, 2007.

Presidential candidate Huckabee's remarks were a refreshing surprise, coming in these days when American budgets favor whopping allocations to national defense or the need to put a man on the latest available planet, but with hardly a nod to the arts.

We must be prepared to make the case for the arts in two needed areas: as a help in improving academics, and its indispensable role in helping our young people escape harrowing social problems.

These healing effects can now be observed on every continent of the globe. A current example is the remarkable Venezuelan Simón Bolívar Youth Orchestra which is currently touring the world. This two-hundred member ensemble called "El Sistema," is now the jewel of the Venezuelan educational program. In this remarkable format, children can begin music lessons at the age of two years. Simon Rattle, famed conductor of the Berlin Philharmonic Orchestra, calls the Venezuelan "Sistema" the most important thing happening in classical music in the world.

Founded in 1975 by organist, economist and politician José Antonio Abreu, the orchestra had its first meeting with eleven children convening in a Caracas parking garage. The ensemble currently numbers two hundred. Joshua Weilerstein, a violinist at the New England Conservatory, comments:

"I think American musicians are incredibly enthusiastic, but there isn't a desperation about the way we play. (The Venezuelans) play as if their lives depend on every note. There's complete passion."[*]

The administration of Hugo Chavez funds most of the $29 million dollars to support the program, and now the "System" boasts some 250,000 members who study in nearly 250 "nucleos" (sites) and play in scores of orchestras. Truly significant are the so-

*From "Sounds of Inspirations" *The Christian Science Monitor,* November 2, 2007. p. 11.

cializing effects on the young orchestra members, and this is what we particularly wish to stress here. The program has served as a family for many, providing them with feelings of hope, bonding and a sense of accomplishment. According to Igor Lanz, executive director of the foundation that oversees El Sistema,

Very early on, the members are equipped with excellent values and a feeling of accomplishment and solidarity by being so extraordinarily involved in music. They are prepared to be better citizens for society.[*]

The orchestra's director, Gustavo Dudamel, who will direct the Los Angeles Philharmonic in 2009, corroborates this feeling of cohesiveness.

In Venezuela, the most important thing is the orchestra. You create a community, a shared objective.

The United States is currently uncomfortable with the socialist trends of the Chavez Venezuelan government. In citing a refusal to be alienated by American prejudices, however, its leader, Churchill is clear.

With relations between the U.S. and Chavez administration often tense—and given Chavez's avowed Anti-Americanism—shunning the U.S. in favor of European venues might have been more expedient. But Churchill believes that "music will transcend" political discord and "be a model for harmonious relations."[**]

"*Theatre as Spiritual Bridge-builder*" is a phrase we might introduce to any potential sponsor. We must be prepared to con-

*Ibid., 13.
**Ibid., 13.

vince the political figure and the educator that the arts inspire a harmonizing effect in which international relationships thrive.

In 1983 The Richard Morse Mime Theatre was chosen to represent America at the Rekjavik, Iceland, Theatre Festival. In arriving in the city, our car was recognized and violently pummeled, accompanied by chants of "*Yankee go home!*" After our performance several nights later, however, there was unalloyed enthusiasm, and during the ensuing evenings with the Icelandic community, we enjoyed moving gatherings with our hosts where we felt soulful connections.

There were many such incidents during our visits to twenty-eight nations. In a 1977 tour, we were scheduled to play in Jerusalem. Though miraculously causing no damage, a bomb had exploded in the square the day before. We were offered the chance to cancel the program by our Israeli hosts, but our group decided to go ahead. That day Israelis and Palestinians stood side by side in the huge town square, enjoying our show in peaceful solidarity. In a memorable moment after the show, an elderly Palestinian, one hand grasping a knotty branch of a cane, and the other the tiny hand of his grandson, limped his way toward me through the crowd. Relinquishing the hand of his grandson, his gnarled hand wrung mine and he pleaded fervently, "You come back! You come back!"

Know what theatre programs have been in place at the institution you are proposing to serve. Has there ever been an acting class in this institution? A dance class? A musical ensemble? Were they effective? If not, why not? *Are there teachers in the school who have shown an interest in participating in such a program?* There is nothing like added help in building a base.

Be aware of community sensibilities. Are there pitfalls that might offend the community? When unscripted theatre is presented for the public, there can be profanity. Here is a rather sad account of the sort of thing which happens repeatedly.

A November 1996 edition of the *St. Louis Post Dispatch* featured a story on its front page that involved a drama teacher who lost her job when her students used profanity in presenting their show. The day after the show, the superintendent's phone was ringing off the hook. The community was enraged. The teacher was dismissed, producing a messy legal case where the teacher sued the board, and the entire theatre program was canceled. A trial lasted four days, after which the board had to pay the dismissed teacher a total of $750,000 and reinstate her. As of this writing, the school board is appealing the decision. But who wins in this situation? No one, really. Though the teacher won the case, the larger question remains: would the school board ever consider another theatre program? And the students were deprived of an activity which, had it been more carefully handled, could have helped them in so many ways.

6. The final suggestion I would make is <u>the necessity of having more than one classroom option available.</u> Many educators can empathize with Beth Murray whose lament is expressed in her 1998 Ph.D. dissertation, *Nowhere to Hide but Together*.

> *Why didn't I know about David Booth?* (author of Story Drama interviewed in Chapter 7) *I also wish I had knowledge of a couple [of] "how to" drama books, like Teaching Drama (Morgan and Saxton. 1987) or Making Sense of Drama (Neelands. 1984). Books like this could have illuminated the complicated intricacies and illustrated the array of options available to the teacher using drama.*[*]

*Murray, *Nowhere to Hide but Together*.

I have been in a similar position on more than one occasion. Here is an account of one such moment.

During the year of 2001–2002, I was approached to teach theatre workshops with young men in the Pere Marquette Detention Center in Grafton, Illinois. Sociology Professor Robert Pennamon of Principia College had organized these workshops which, I was advised, should include movement exercises to free their capacities for body expression. There were seventeen in the workshop, consisting of young men from many racial backgrounds.

I was three weeks into this program, and things were not going well. I couldn't figure it out. In fact, I was so discouraged that I was on the brink of "throwing in the towel." I had volunteered to do a mime program which the authorities thought would be great fun for the teenage boys. From the first session, however, I was taken aback by what presented itself as a disconcerting lack of interest. I couldn't get *anywhere!* I would begin a session, and the boys sprawled around like wet noodles out of the water. Their eyes drooped, and they appeared to have lost their spines. I was really concerned, and even felt that I was losing my grip.

As I entered the administrative office before the fourth session, however, I bumped into the detention center supervisor, who asked me how things were going. Feeling embarrassed, I told him of my problem, that I felt I was failing to animate the boys, and would understand if he wanted to cancel the program. The director shrugged and smiled, saying, "Well, you know, don't you, that the guys have been playing non-stop basketball for two and a half hours before they get to you. And then they have a big dinner?"

Hell-o-o! I might have been more aware of their schedules before devising the program. I thanked him for enlightening me, took my leave and prepared to enter the class. But the dilemma was, "What *now?*"

I recalled how in New York in what we called "breakthrough sessions," students who were frustrated by life's problems, would suddenly open up when they were encouraged to talk about themselves. These sessions had provided them with the opportunity to talk about their problems, and then we would construct a situation based upon these entanglements in ways that would help them to break free. These sessions resulted in notable transformations.* I mused, "What would happen here if . . . ?" as I gathered up my notebook to join the boys.

As I entered the class, I was again greeted by heavy eyelids and sagging bodies. Instead of using a movement-based program, we drew up the chairs in a circle and began to talk together.

Sitting in a circle for the first time, the boys started to talk about their lives. They shared information on their backgrounds, including whatever had led them to incarceration. On the surface it appeared little more than a "bull session." But the truth was that the boys were listening to each other supportively. The session gathered momentum and took on a new life. Bonding was taking place that hadn't appeared before. Some boys really loved giving advice, and would hardly stop in their roles as counselors.

By the next week I had a new program in place in which we would use these personal stories as the basis of exercises. I encouraged the boys to continue talking about their problems with their home lives, with the law, with their schools—anything they wanted. After a couple of weeks, I asked them to write about all this. Soon they were turning out stories and poems which we would share together. I was surprised to see how many chose to write poetry. The third stage came when I asked if they would like to act these events out in original scenes. This they did with some extraordinary results.

Moving and insightful moments surfaced during that year, such as the improvising of imaginary appearances before parole boards. Often release from the center depended on these inter-

*See the account of Ramos in the "Prisons" section in Part III of this book

views, and the parole officials were not known for a patience with hesitancy and shyness. The class provided a possibility in preparing for these encounters. One boy who struggled with chronic shyness showed himself to be inadequately prepared for such an interview with the board that was to take place in ten days. The boys all commented on his lack of preparedness and his almost inaudible voice. When he repeated the exercise before an imaginary interrogator, played by one of his classmates, what a difference! The boys in the workshop were developing the muscles of confidence before our eyes.

I'll mention just one other case where a moving change happened with a young man.

Eduardo, about sixteen or seventeen, was initially extremely resistant to the workshop. For weeks he was a surly observer, but I never insisted that he participate. Then suddenly one night he jumped into the discussion in a big way.

It happened like this: One boy, Julio, stated that he didn't know if he could resist rejoining the drug trade once on the outside. But Eduardo, who had seen his own family virtually destroyed through addiction, suddenly exploded! He had *plenty* to say. Julio was simply overwhelmed!

At the final session all the boys formed a line at the door to say goodbye to me. Eduardo made a point of waiting until I had shaken hands with all the others. I wondered what was on his mind. At the end of the line and now facing me, he said, "Thank you, Richard. I didn't understand you at first. But you helped me. You helped all of us. Thank you, Richard!"

It was a handshake I shall never forget.

*   *   *

As an addendum to this chapter, and in the great tradition of TIE practice, I offer two dramatic dialogs to illustrate two aspects of "bridge building" touched upon in this chapter. Either scene, or both, may strike the reader as a bit frivolous, but I take this risk of departing from the more august path we have been following in permitting an alternate approach to serious matters. They have to do with differing aspects of advocacy. The first is based upon fact, and has to do with fundraising. I hope that it might be helpful to those who are engaged in trying to attract financial support for their organization. The second scene is fictitious and has to do with cementing good relationships with the school board, local authorities or civic leaders.

In the 70's, The Richard Morse Mime Theatre like most non-profit theatre companies, urgently needed help from the outside. As everyone who has directed a theatre company knows, only a fraction of the expenses of the company can be made up through ticket sales, or activities such as soliciting ads from local merchants to be printed in the theatre programs. On repeated occasions I had to meet with business executives, bank presidents or airline executives in hope of attracting corporate support. A workshop offered by the Theatre Communications Group of New York City designed to bolster savvy and confidence in the petitioner was helpful. Here is a record based on my first interview, which I can tell you made me at least as nervous as any audition I had ever faced.

I was to approach the "Stoddard Foundation" to attract funding for The Richard Morse Mime Theatre in the 1970's. One factor that was emphasized in the advisory sessions was the importance of knowing what you and your prospective donor have in common. Some of this information is available in publications of donor organizations.

SCENE: GETTING THE ATTENTION OF
BIG BUSINESS

(The names of the CEO and of his corporation have been altered until this account can be, in the frequently employed words of an American administration not to be named, "de-classified").

I entered the luxuriously furnished office of CEO Channing of the Stoddard Foundation. The first rule is to let your interviewer take the lead, and trust that you will know what to say and when. On Channing's shelf, behind his chair, there were pictures of his *children, animals, sports heroes, a Boston Red Sox cap, and a Harvard diploma.*

I entered and sat down.

CEO Channing: Hi, Richard. So nice to meet you. We've heard great things about your work.

Richard: Thanks, Mr. Channing.

C: How did you happen to go into mime, Richard?

R: Well, you see, when I was growing up in BOSTON, I was into athletics . . .

C: Oh, you come from Boston?

R: Oh, yes, from an old New England family. And growing up there I developed this love of movement from SPORTS, you see.

C: Oh, I'm from that area myself. Where did you grow up?

R: Actually from Newton.

C: Newton! Oh, yes. Lovely section, Newton. But I didn't realize that you came from a sports background.

R: Oh, yes, I practically lived at Fenway Park during the baseball season. We'd yell ourselves hoarse as kids rooting for the RED SOX.

C: The Red Sox! Well I can see that we have things in common.

R: You mean that you come from New England, too?

C: Oh, yes. I transferred here from the NECCO candy company.

R: You mean in Newtonville? On the Charles River? Why I used to visit there all the time. My friend's father was an executive there.

C: Who was that?

R: His name was . . . let me remember . . . oh, yes. Ray Potter.

C: Really, Ray worked for us for years. He was a lovely man.

R: He used to do this woodworking on the side. I'll never forget the day he made a little boat for me in his office. He was certainly a kind person. (all true)

C: So you're a Sox fan?

R: I practically lived in the center field bleachers. You see, my grandfather was sports editor of the Boston Herald *for many years, and now he has a plaque in the Cooperstown Hall of Fame. (also true)*

C: Well, for goodness sake!

R: Yeah. He went into sports writing just after graduating from HARVARD.

C: Harvard? I graduated there in 1960.

R: That's something. I attended HARVARD myself one summer. I remember those days seeing the Harvard-Yale games at Harvard Stadium.

C: What memories! Did you ever hear Tom Lehrer's song about the Harvard team?

R: Remember it well. (singing)

> *Fight fiercely Harvard, fight, fight, fight!*
> *Demonstrate to them your will.*
> *Although their boys may have the might*
> *Our boys possess the skill . . .*

C and R together:

> *How we will celebrate our victory!*
> *We'll have the whole team out to tea!*
> *Fight fiercely, Harvard, fight, fight, fight!*
> *To vic-to-reeeee!*

C: Hey not bad! Not bad!!!

R: Oh, yes, those were happy days. We used to go in a group and root for Cronin, Williams, the lot. Ha! I'll never forget the day I shook hands with Ted Williams. I wouldn't wash my hands for a week! And then I was introduced to Joe DiMaggio when I was fourteen.

C: That's amazing. You could write a book about all that, I think.

163

R: Well . . . Now where did you grow up?

C: Cambridge. On Brattle Street.

R: Brattle *Street! Why that's where I spent the other half of my life! At the Brattle Street Theatre. They did these shows for children and that's where I first became interested in CHILDREN'S THEATRE. And now we have this great theatre for kids.*

C: Yes, I heard you have a children's theatre and your company does a lot with special audiences.

R: Well, we do what we can. We do performances for special groups during the week . . . like SLOAN-KETTERING.

C: Sloan-Kettering? Why that's one of the chief causes we support.

R: Really? We've been three times now. (true)

C: Now, we've never sponsored a theatre group before. But . . . tell me about your shows.

R: Well, they're basically very funny shows. We have numbers from everyday life that the kids love. And there's always something that calls attention to special issues. Like kindness to ANIMALS.

C: Animals, why that's lovely. Our kids love *animals! What do you do?*

R: We have these beautiful masks—a lion, an elephant—the numbers sensitize kids to animals. And the kids can actually pet them . . . Might I ask if you have children?

C: Two. Tanya is 12 and Billy is 10.

R: Now, why don't you all come to our theatre down on Waverly Place in the Village Saturday. We'll save four tickets, and your kids will have a terrific time.

C: Do you have space for my wife?

R: Of course! Adults love the show as much as the kids.

C: Well, thank you, Richard.

R: We'd love to have her with us. (marking it down) O.K. You have four tickets for this Saturday. The show is called Mixed Nuts.

C: Ha . . . ha . . . ha! That sounds like fun!

R: Yes. It's a lot of fun. Audiences love it . . . Here's a flyer with the address and show time. The tickets will be at the box office. The show starts at 2. If you can be there early, we have a little party before the performance. And when we play for hospitals, we take the party with us.

C: That's great! (looking over brochure) This interests me . . . And would you be willing to play again at Sloan-Kettering?

R: Absolutely we'll . . . Just come Saturday with your wife and children. And meet all the actors after.

C: Great! Thank you, Richard. We'll be there. . . . Richard, it's great meeting you!

R: Me, too, Mr. Channing. I think you'll have a great time. I'm leaving the TIMES *Review of our show with some brief information on our company.*

C: Fine, Richard. I'll look this over . . . O.K., Richard. We'll be there.

R: (rising) A great *pleasure, Mr. Channing. See you Saturday!*

Once the family had visited, the idea was sold because the kids had a ripping time, and the CEO, who had usually sent his kids to the movies or some such entertainment, became hooked on our theatre. The following Monday I had a call from his secretary. We were receiving a grant in the amount of $5,000.00, a royal sum in those days.

The second scene illustrates how a skilled "psychologist" with more than enough chutzpah can further the cause of TIE in an interview with a high school principal.

Scene Two

Here, Dolly Duff (aka Dolly Levi [pace Thornton Wilder]) Attacks Dr. Schultz, Principal of Short Falls High.

Friday afternoon at the office of Principal Schultz at Short Falls High. Dr. Cyrus Schultz is hard at work with budget figures. Something must be cut. The high school's theatre department, already marginalized, is a prime candidate. A knock is heard.

Schultz: Come in. . . . (Enter Dolly Duff of the English Department who doubles as the Short Falls Drama Department Director. Dolly is well coiffed and perfumed, and is roughly patterned after Thornton Wilder's irrepressible Dolly Levi in The Matchmaker*) Oh, yes, Ms. Duff . . . I know you wanted to see me. I'm happy that you've come, but I'm afraid I don't have a lot of time.*

Duff: Thank you, Principal Schultz, for allowing me to visit. I know how busy you are, and I promise to be brief.

Schultz: Thank you for understanding, Ms. Duff.

Duff: Of course . . . Well, first, I have to tell you how enthused we all are about the work you're doing. The new schedule is just a brilliant idea!

Schultz: (taken aback) Oh. Oh, really. Thank you. That's nice of you to be so supportive. A principal doesn't always hear praise like that! (He laughs; she laughs.)

Duff: Of course. Now, Principal Schultz, I'll come right to the point. You know The Short Falls Drama Club is working hard on these scenes that they're presenting on Parents' Night in two weeks.

Schultz: Yes, and we're all looking forward to that. How's it coming along? Uh . . . uh, I do hear a lot of noise out of SG 206 at four o'clock. (flashing orange alert for Ms. Duff).

Duff: That's part of what I want to explain. You see, the students are so enthused in doing this program and at times it's hard to restrain their joy.

Schultz: Joy? (Joy, here?)

Duff: Oh, yes. Why one of the mothers called me the other day, and said she's never seen her daughter so happy. (Leaning toward Schultz and lowering her voice) Dr. Schultz, she even insisted on being at school last Monday when she had a cold!

Schultz: No! (pondering a potential remedy for mounting absenteeism). Could that be true?

Duff: Oh yes, and the attendance records are up twenty-nine percent since we formed the Short Falls Players! ... But there's something else I just want to mention.

Schultz: Something else? (She wants more money for the theatre. Ironically) What could that be, Miss Duff?

Duff: Well, the original plays the students are writing are just fascinating, and I think the parents will be so proud of their kids. But in the course of the plays, there might be ... just might be ... well, some occasional "rough talk." You know like what the young people might hear in the streets. There might be a little of that. I just wanted to mention this to you. But it really shouldn't ...

Schultz: (interrupting) Now, see here, Ms. Duff, I'm afraid I can't encourage you there. You see, in addition to our own staff and parents, there will be people from the outside. I mean administrators who are assessing what we do here ... And you know they control our funding.

Duff: Exactly. And that's why I wanted to discuss this with you. You see, I can talk to the kids and explain that if they want the drama program—which they are so enthused about—they can cut any profanity.

Schultz: Well, I'm afraid they'll have to.

Duff: Fine. Don't worry about it. And now I have a plan. Would you allow me to say a few words at the faculty meeting Monday?

Schultz: Well, we don't have much time, but ... well, we'll see. I do appreciate that . . . All right, I'll give you five minutes if you'll be brief.

Duff: Of course. I just want to announce how well the program is coming on and thank everybody for their support for the drama club.

Schultz: That's a good point. We certainly don't want any more parents' letters in the Pilot like we had after Grease *last year . . . Phew! That almost did us in!*

Duff: Right! I agree! I'm with you. So my final request is that you attend the Monday rehearsal with any of the school board that you'd like to invite. Then, if you really object to anything, anything at all, we can discuss it.

Schultz: Well, that's very considerate. I just don't know. Let me think about it.

Duff: I will leave it up to you. We don't want to offend anyone. The kids all love the program. . . . (Casually, as she gathers her things and starts for the door) And isn't it wonderful that the National Endowment is coming to the opening performance? (A real life Dolly Levi.)

Schultz: The what? The National Endowment is . . . ? What, coming here?

Duff: Yes. Didn't you get my notice? I received a note from the NEA and the State Council that they're both coming to the show?

Schultz: Notice? . . . Well, I've been kind of busy . . .

Duff: Yes, the NEA representative is coming. I already told him that the grades of all the students in the group are improving by about thirty-four percent since the program began last year, according to Mr. Gatsby, our English teacher. He's even made a study based on the theatre's effect on student grades this last year. . . . And here, here is the latest documentation from the NEA in Washington on how drama is improving student grades nationwide in subjects like history, math and science. Look. The SAT scores with drama students are forty-one percent higher!

Schultz: Forty-one percent! Forty-one . . . what?

Duff: Forty-one percent higher than before the program! But here, you can read it for yourself. Here's an extra copy I just happen to have with me of The Stanford-based Shirley Brice Heath Report documenting that (reading) "those involved in theatre programs score forty-one percent higher in the SATs than students involved in conventional study methods. And they also rate higher in intra-personal relationships." That means they get better jobs after graduation, Dr. Schultz. I know that Dr. Lewis of the assessment team here at Short Falls will really take an interest in that!

Schultz: That's quite remarkable . . . Forty-one percent? . . . Are you sure? I mean I didn't know about the Stamford . . . the Stamford . . . what?

Duff: Stanford! The California STANFORD report . . . which is recognized as doing some of the most significant research work in the country. It's so exciting what they're finding . . . But it's all here. Just read this (pulling out an extra copy of The Shirley Brice Heath Report from her handbag.) It's all certified. Here . . . Ooooh! (her body trembling) It gives me goose bumps! I can't wait to read the "Short Falls Alumni Purpose" a year from now! I can just see the reports on our graduates.

Schultz: (taking pamphlet from Instructor Duff) Well, this is all very interesting. I didn't realize that drama was doing all that.

Duff: Oh, yes. I almost forgot. Did you know that PS 147 is now considering a program like ours? They noticed how our program has been so effective in reducing crime in the neighborhood.

Schultz: Reducing crime? . . . How on earth does drama do that?!

Duff: Yes, yes! No doubt about it. You see, it's all very simple. This program provides our young people with something to do in their after school hours. And somewhere to go. They are off the streets at night. They're rehearsing, sewing costumes, building sets, learning publicity, selling ads for the program, baking cookies for opening nights. They're involved! . . . And now for the first time in years, their parents are attending PTA meetings!

Schultz: Yes? . . . Well, that's great . . . I hadn't realized that . . .

Duff: Oh, yes, yes. And this has all been owing to the program that you authorized. And everyone's beginning to notice . . . Why we could be establishing a national trend right here at little Short Falls High . . . We . . . we . . . Dr. Schultz?

Schultz: (musing on his acceptance speech at the coming Short Falls April awards dinner after being elected "Innovative Educator of the Year".) Uh . . . uh . . . sorry. Well, I must say, you make me feel good. So many on the staff seem critical about what I do here. Thank you for noticing.

Duff: Noticing?! Who isn't noticing?! This is your program. It just couldn't have taken place without your imagination, your vision, and everybody knows that!

171

Schultz: (reddening a bit) Well . . . well, I . . . I . . .

Duff: Well. (recognizing that she has the momentum and, as actors well know, timing the exit on a high note is essential) Well, I know how busy you are, Dr. Schultz. (gathering her handbag and rising) So I can count on you to come to rehearsal on Monday?

Schultz: Well . . . if you think the kids wouldn't mind . . .

Duff: Mind? Mind! Why the kids are so excited that you might look in.

Schultz: Really . . . Well . . . yes . . . Well . . . yes . . . this sounds . . . (now hearing his name echoing over the Washington Mall as he is summoned to the dais to receive the plaque in recognition of his new title, this time as "National Educator of the Year.")

Duff: (casually humming the strains of "Stars and Stripes Forever" in gathering her coat) Then, Dr. Schultz? . . . Uh, Dr. Schultz? . . .

Schultz: (waking) Oh . . . oh sorry. I'm sorry . . .

Duff: Remember, Monday at 4 in the auditorium?

Schultz: Yes . . . Well . . . yes . . . good . . . ("Stars and Stripes" segues into deafening applause and flashing fireworks. Schultz is now lost in reverie as he stares at his bookcase contemplating where he might make space for the new plaque.)

Duff: Dr. Schultz . . . Dr. Schultz . . . are you all right?

Schultz: Uh . . . uh . . . Oh, sorry, Ms. Duff . . . Well (smiling euphorically) . . . yes . . . Thank you, thank you, Ms. Duff.

Duff: Toodle-oo-oo, Dr. Schultz!

(Dolly Duff leaves office, as Schultz rises and begins to make space on the third shelf.)

FIN

As Dolly Duff departs, let's acknowledge that this scenario is susceptible of many possibilities, such as a resounding "NO!" from Principal Schultz. But, recalling that fortune favors the bold, let us also recognize that with a little bit of imagination . . . and luck . . .

"Anything can be negotiated!"

Part III

A History for Tomorrow

NINE

SHAMANISM

"The Programs are helping kids in school as well as getting those who have dropped out back into school."

—Judith Humphrey Weitz[*]

Every educator involved with theatre's potential for healing benefits from a knowledge of its healing traditions. One of these is shamanism. This ancient healing art holds ample riches for us today. The rewards of such knowledge are not found in attempting to emulate the transformative methods of ancient tribal leaders (historians agree that the ceremonies of shamanism necessarily varied with each tribe), but rather to convert them into creative methods that can benefit our students today. Ancient shamanic rites usually employed extensive exercises in whirling and dancing conducted over long periods of time. Certainly the modern teacher would find these practices well out of reach.

But once we have understood the *intentions* of shamanism and the guiding methods that drove it, *we are free to create our own derivative exercises that will accomplish the same objectives sought by these ancient healers.* This may seem presumptuous, but it is not. We honor any tradition by adapting its principles in ways available to us in our own times. If we can grasp, for example, that the basis of

*Weitz, *Coming Up Taller*.

shamanic healing is rooted in *bonding* and *inclusion*, we can be liberated to create our own effective programs that will generate this community connection with our students today. (A proven example of this kind of adaptation appears at the end of this chapter.)

Anthropologists tell us that the practice of shamanism has existed since the Paleolithic, or Stone Age, and we know that it is still practiced on every continent today. In indigenous community life, the shaman was historically the tribal leader, and equally respected as seer, prophet, source of spiritual wisdom and healer. It is the office of "healer" that clearly identifies the man or woman designated as the tribal shaman. Anthropologist Henry Munn records a self-proclaimed definition of a shaman:

> *I am he who puts together, he who speaks, he who searches. I am he who looks for the spirit of the day. I search where there is fright and terror, I am he who fixes, he who cures the person that is sick.* [*]

While the use of herbs or other material methods may be employed in shamanic rites, it is mainly through effecting a *change of consciousness* that the patient, referred to as the celebrant, is freed from imprisoning physical or mental bondage. In a classic sequence of shamanic healing, the patient is first urged to whirl and dance to the accompaniment of a drum or flute for long periods of time, encircled by supportive clan members. This strenuous exercise leads to a state of exhaustion, wherein the celebrant yields all attachment to present life and submits to the guiding influence of the shaman. This achieved, a dream state is induced by the shaman healer in which the clan member departs on an imaginary journey. This dream excursion, referred to as a "rite of passage," can in-

*Munn, Henry, "The Mushrooms of Language in Hallucinogens and Shamanism," as quoted by Joan Halifax, *Shamanic Voices.* The Penguin Group: 1979. (3)

volve embarking on a hazardous river voyage, or penetrating a dark forest. Eminent mythologist Joseph Campbell describes the nature of this mental journey:

> *Once having traversed the threshold, the hero (or the celebrant in shamanic rite) moves in a dream landscape of curiously fluid, ambiguous forms, where he must survive a succession of trials.* [*]

The voyages of Homer exemplify this kind of journey where the hero also must survive a series of hazardous ordeals. Classic theatre also abounds with examples, such as in the *Oedipus Rex* of Sophocles, or in Shakespeare's *King Lear*. In each of these dramatic works, the trials of a perilous voyage are the "rite of passage" leading the hero to higher self-awareness.

Modern literature also abounds with examples of this ritualized journey where protagonists must survive an anguished inner voyage in atoning for their sins. Consider, for example, Charles Dickens' classic tale, *A Christmas Carol*. In the course of a dream, the "celebrant," Scrooge, is escorted by his former business partner, Jacob Marley, through a series of agonizing nocturnal journeys which force Scrooge to confront his inordinate greed in a manner that real life cannot supply.

In analyzing how theatre heals, theatre historians seem to find common ground. Most start with Aristotle's definition of tragedy, which includes this passage:

> *Tragedy, then, is an imitation of an action that is serious, complete, and of a certain magnitude; . . . through pity and fear effecting the proper purgation of these emotions.* [**]

---

*Campbell, *The Hero with a Thousand Faces*, 18.
**Aristotle, *Politics* (viii), 7.

Aristotle then connects this process of purgation with catharsis, defined in part by Webster as "the relieving of the emotions by art," in another passage of the *Poetics*:

> *Any feeling which comes strongly to some exists in all others to a greater or less degree, pity and fear, for example, but also this "enthusiasm." . . . And those who feel pity or fear or other emotions must be affected in just the same way to the extent that the emotion comes upon each. To them all comes a pleasant feeling of purgation and relief.*[*]

The passage implies that the spectator empathizes with another's predicament to such a degree that the spectator's own problems diminish and dissolve. Mythologist Joseph Campbell writes:

> *Furthermore, we have not even to risk the adventure alone, for the heroes of all time have gone before us. The labyrinth is thoroughly known. We have only to follow the thread of the hero path, and where we had thought to find an abomination, we shall find a god. And where we had thought to slay another, we shall slay ourselves. Where we had thought to travel outward, we will come to the center of our own existence. And where we had thought to be alone, we will be with all the world.*[**]

The assurance is that *we are not alone* is at the comforting center of theatre's healing process. An interesting analysis of this process wherein we are purged, and one not without humor, is provided by noted scholar, J. Michael Walton in his *Tragedy Reviewed: The Greek Sense of Theatre:*

---

[*]Sinclair, T.A., Trans. of Aristotle, *Politics, (Viii)*, 1962, (7)
[**]Campbell, *The Power of Myth*, 123.

Catharsis has become almost a synonym for "recreation." Plato had admitted the need for recreation in order to restore the emotional balance. Aristotle allows the theatre as this recreational function and welcomes, with suitable safeguards, a theatre which can deeply affect its audience. . . . The audience feels sympathy with the stage characters and achieves a release of emotional tension by weeping on their behalf. Or to reduce the argument from the sublime, we would be entitled to think that Aristotle might have applauded the sentiment of Ogden Nash that

> *Virtue's noble and Vice is vile*
> *But you need an orgy once in a while.*

The theatre as orgy, then: or perhaps, as an experience, the watching of tragedy is a kind of spiritual emetic, contributing to the sanity and balance of individual and community. [*]

For one traveling in Greece, it is interesting to note the geographical inseparability of theatre and temple. In most cases, the theatre occupies a superior position, as is evident at major cities such as Epidaurus and Delphi. This proximity symbolizes the indissoluble spiritual partnership which has historically connected worship, theatre and healing. Noted therapist Pat Watts, who has studied this healing-theatre relationship in great detail, comments:

At Epidaurus, the amphitheatre was next door or may have been part of the complex of the clinic of Aesculapius (the healing god of Greek mythology). The participation as audience in the plays was part of the cure. Perhaps people attended the theatre to experience the presence of the god. They did not go to be entertained or diverted. [**]

*[*]Walton, *Tragedy Reviewed*, 25, 26.
[**]Jennings, *Dramatherapy*, 48.

The rites of Shamanism and those of the ancient Greek theatre were based upon a mutually accepted shape, that of the circle. In the ceremony of shamanism, the patient, or "celebrant," was thought to have wandered beyond the circle of community connection. The shaman exerted mighty efforts to return the victim back within it, and this return symbolized the completion of the healing rite. The circle shape of the ancient Greek Theatre united actor and audience, implying a shared experience. As Sue Jennings and Ase Minde have indicated in their book, *Art Therapy and Dramatherapy: Masks of the Soul:*

> *The circle shape was also an inherited concept of the ancient Greek theatre which united audience and actors. The theatre circle of ancient Greece itself was conceived as a healing space. Or as art therapist, Sue Jennings remarks: "The circular shapes that we refer to . . . were once the sacred spaces that contained the healing theatre."*[*]

In her book titled *Calling the Circle, the First and Future Culture,* author Christina Baldwin describes how the power of the circle retains its eternal capacity to restore peaceful bonding with humankind today.

> *The circle, even when highly focused on task, operates as a bonded community. First, as we are introducing ourselves, the Peer-Spirit structure provides a matrix upon which we can depend. Our first bond is to the structure. Then, as we progress into our work together, the structure fosters within each of us a respect that bonds us to each other. This bonding is something many of us seek. One of the ways we measure success in the circle is that we grow in commitment and loyalty to each other as we work through inter-*

*Jennings and Minde, *Art Therapy and Dramatherapy*, 94.

personal issues while accomplishing intention. For most of us, the interpersonal structure is an additional draw to the circle form.[*]

The circle is being explored by an increasing number of teachers today. In many visits to his classes, I was continually intrigued by the ways in which Dr. Colin Campbell of Principia College employed the circle to dynamic effect in his teaching process. As Dr. Campbell explained to me:

I try to get the students to understand human motives, behavior values as an actor would. The idea is to create a collective sense. The experience is as close to self-education as possible. The composition is seen as a play. The centerpiece is all the students' performance. I put them in a circle. We go around the circle. If one doesn't know the answer, I have them "piggy-back" on others' answers. Feelings come into it by not allowing them to say, "I can't do it."

I urge them all to take acting![**]

An interesting moment occurred in the summer of 1977 that helped me to appreciate this fascinating subject of theatre and healing. Three of us, Rasa Allan, Gabriel Barre and I, represented The Richard Morse Mime Theatre, and we were concluding a State Department-sponsored performance tour of twelve countries. Our last stop was Greece where we performed in some remote mountainous settings as well as in urban centers, such as Athens. We were also invited to perform in a series of orphanages in the far off villages of Volos and Joannina in Thessalonika. Many of these children had survived indescribably tragic war experiences in the 70's. Some had witnessed their parents dragged from their beds at night, never to be heard of again. But now for

*Baldwin, Christina, 1994. (189)
**Colin Campbell, interview with author, September 12, 2003.

these moments, we could be together, and they felt cared for. They looked on in rapt wonder, and the heavenly sounds of their delighted laughter was a highlight of our tour.

Our tour accomplished, we decided to vacation for a few days on the Greek island of Kos, the reputed birthplace of the healing God, Aesculapius.

One day we hiked to the site of the ancient theatre with a Greek friend whom we had met on the island. The theatre was in ruins, but two large weather-polished stones that had endured the winds and rains of twenty-three centuries, marked the entrance. On each of these time-worn boulders was a long series of carved inscriptions. Upon questioning our friend, a native of the island, about their meaning, he replied nonchalantly, "Oh, these are the recorded accounts of the healings that took place during the performances."

Can the transforming "circle of inclusion" be put to use in the contemporary classroom? For today's educator, this is well worth exploring, as Professor Colin Campbell has done.

Here let me describe a simple theatre exercise based on the shamanic circle which I found helpful in creating bonds of assurance and connection.

Many schools today have no provision for a theatre program. There is usually no funding to support an arts program. But the educator should not accept defeat. We must look for the window of opportunity, and just a few minutes, once or twice a week given to a theatre exercise, can work wonders in lifting classroom morale.

For years I conducted workshops in New York which we called "Breakthrough" sessions. These were aimed at releasing emotions through various exercises. They became popular in New York and we added extra sessions on Saturdays which gave us more time together. The same happened later in the 90's with students at Principia College.

Here is one exercise we used in "Breakthrough" which can be

readily put to use by any teacher who wishes to try it. It can also be adapted to virtually any classroom or dance studio space.

Description

Time: This exercise can be accomplished in about twenty to thirty minutes, though more time is useful when available.

Objectives: To stimulate a connection between all students; to break down the walls of shyness; to encourage initiative; to stimulate feelings of joy in the classroom.

Space requirements: A clean floor space where all may move freely.

Dress: Loose fitting apparel to permit free movement. Sweatshirts or T shirts; slacks or sweat pants are fine. A light sneaker, slipper or dance shoe is preferred.

Equipment for teacher: A cassette or CD player that can be easily controlled.

A small hand drum, or tambourine.

Music: Choose music from a tape or CD which is lively but not heavy. Choose a sound that will be easy for the group to follow. Something that suggests a light lyricism or humor is fine. It should not be fast, aggressive, or contrapuntal, but music which has a gently steady beat which enables all to join in. We found the lyrical pieces of Melissa Manchester favorable; some of the upbeat bizouki rhythms of the Greek music of Hadjidakis were also helpful in creating a lightly spirited mood.

Now try to picture the following sequence. You are the leader—the designated shaman.

185

1) Ask the students to space themselves freely around the studio allowing ample space between bodies. Put on the music, and invite them to move about the room to the rhythm of the selection, moving in any *direction* they like. Encourage an easy "free style" manner in allowing the students to feel the music. They can be free to walk, jump, roll on the floor—anything. Continue for several minutes. Let all move freely with no criticism. <u>If some don't participate, let this pass.</u> They will often be attracted to join later.

2) Next, announce that you would like everyone to form a circle with plenty of space between them. Go to the center, and invite the students to walk clockwise in response to a regular tempo that you have chosen. From this point, you are the leader, so demonstrate everything you wish them to do, using the music, or your hand drum, or whatever. Repeat counter-clockwise. Keeping the circle large to avoid collisions, have the students run lightly with an easy bounce, not covering too much ground. Urge them to enjoy the process of moving. Preserve the rhythm and the space between the individuals, and remind them to keep the circle wide as it tends to close in. Continue this light running, then introduce kicking the legs in rhythm, forward and back, as they continue to move in the circle. After a few measures, announce a change of direction.

Return to walking; add longer strides, with vigorous arm swings still preserving a good spatial relationship between participants. Try to keep the rhythms even, working with counts of four or eight, which are easy time structures to follow. (You may eventually prescribe other rhythms, such as that of a waltz, but not for a while.)

3) Without breaking the rhythm of the previous section, call for a participant in the class to step to the center of the circle, and for a few moments invite this individual to become the leader. Ask them to move intuitively in any shape or rhythm they wish the oth-

186

ers to follow. Emphasize <u>the need to communicate movement patterns clearly to the rest of the group.</u>

This is a simple example of how connection can be cultivated. The individual is encouraged to communicate the pattern to the group, and the leader receives visual corroboration that s/he is or is not successful.

<u>Watch for problems.</u> *If the leader gets a little too wild and hard to follow, allow them to thrash about for a while before suggesting that they communicate a pattern that allows the others to follow. In future sessions, you will see this individual gradually harmonizing with the group without your urging. This can be a vital moment in that individual's growth, as participants become sensitized to their fellow participants.*

Allow each member her or his needed time, and sense when the moment arrives for a change. If each can carry on for a minute or so at the beginning, that's great. If there is acute shyness, be content with progress on a very simple level, praise them, and call for another leader.

<u>Point: Be prepared to encourage anyone who might be having a struggle with leadership.</u> *Use encouragement with simple phrases such as "That's it"... "Now you have it"... "That's better!"... "Go with that!" What you will be seeing in each session is a growing confidence among some of those formerly reticent.* <u>Remember that many have not done anything like this leadership exercise before.</u> *The joy of the class and the laughter which inevitably arises should help to draw them into the center of the circle more successfully. You are building initiative, and some who have never ever been a leader in their lives, will gain confidence in developing the muscles of authority. Work with the idea that whatever they come up with is terrific!*

Continue until everyone has had an opportunity to lead the group, taking pains never to force or embarrass anyone who feels reticent. They'll probably join in eventually (as did Geoffrey in Chapter Four), if you have succeeded in creating an atmosphere of play.

> Remember two things: *(1) keep the feeling of exuberant play uppermost at this stage of the workshop and (2) praise everyone who comes into the center for* <u>something</u> *they are doing!*

Never miss the opportunity to praise freely through all this part of the work. For some this might be the first time in their lives that they have felt encouragement from another, including family, friends or teachers. You are now building group support, and if you continue this exercise over a period of days, you will begin to see the shy ones "bud and blossom as the rose." Why? Because they are all being included, and they are all being accepted.

> *As you proceed, sense who may require praise the most. If there is any doubt, risk giving more praise and encouragement than is necessary. We usually err on the side of too little in life rather than too much, so never miss the chance to approve of* <u>something</u>. *If someone is struggling, let them alone, then have them repeat the segment later when you can add the approval with words such as* "<u>Much better!</u>" . . . *"Isn't s/he better, class!?" The class will invariably come to the aid of the struggling member at this point, reinforcing the progress. Remember that in encouraging mutual support, you are helping the members to bond with each other, which you will see happen before your eyes.*

When you have built up the positive feelings in a group, you have achieved a great deal. You will have created an atmosphere of inclusion and group support, free from any form of criticism, comparisons, or judgment. (In this regard, never say, of course, "Try to do as Charlie did," "I see it's a problem, but you'll catch on," or anything like that.)

To the struggling child or young person, find an opportunity after the class to take her or him aside privately and tell them how *especially* good they were. <u>Very important.</u>

> *In all this process of encouragement, we see the shaman (you) at work, encouraging, celebrating, and drawing each individual deeper into the circle of connection with the others. Recall that shamanic rites often lasted for days. The important lesson to learn from that, I think, is patience. The shaman healer never gave up on the celebrant until there was a return to the circle, or healing was realized. You are developing this patience even as your pupils are developing their own skills of spontaneity and initiative.*

New teachers should not fear to take on this kind of classroom work. If you have achieved just this one exercise, you will see how much better the day goes and how morale has lifted. We found this inevitable in all our workshops—with K–12 young people, and with advanced students through college years. *I was surprised to hear how many of the college students had never been praised for anything.*

Try to end the session with a few minutes of physical exertion, perhaps repeating some of the beginning warmups. We usually ended on a quiet note, permitting moments of reflection on what had passed. Here we called for silence in joining hands and stretching out to the limits of the circle, then slowly advancing inward toward each other to form a tight nucleus, then expanding, then closing perhaps three or four times. In the final contraction of the circle, you should call for complete silence. Let the final contraction lead to a group embrace, held for a minute or so, or for as long as you feel appropriate. Some of these moments were quite moving, and tears were released as blocked emotions were touched.

Many of the kids, teenagers and the adults could not wait for another session. For some, the opportunity for free corporeal expression was the important part; others enjoyed a shared celebration of their own and the group's achievements; for others it was feeling praise; and for most, if not all, the significant thing was the feeling of connection and bonding the exercise inspired.

For the teacher who has never tried conducting this kind of group exercise, the key lies in the courage to begin. It is helpful to rehearse the sequences you would like to lead in the privacy of your home. Leading an imaginary class can give you the assurance that you can do it. Also, each return to this activity with the group will bring added self-assurance, and you will find yourself improvising with increasing freedom. The shaman/teacher—you—invariably gains from conducting this exercise as well as your class, and the exhilaration of shamanic bonding will remain with you always.

May you find it so!

TEN

MASKS
(DVD disc 2: sections 1 and 2)

We don't necessarily have to revolutionize the theatre. It may be that the best theatre—if it comes—will develop from the most traditional forms. A theatre is good when it makes sense to people.
—Peter Schumann[*]

Masks have been long associated with healing rites in ancient communities. The shaman healers described in the preceding chapter usually wore masks, or if not, their faces were heavily painted. For the theatre educator the mask holds vital lessons in two important areas: as a means of heightening performance expressiveness and as a therapeutic aid.

In 1999–2000, the St. Louis Art Museum, the Chicago Field Museum, and the Houston Museum of Fine Arts, combined to present an extensive exhibition, *Masks: Faces of Culture*. Featuring 139 masks from 68 museums and private collections around the world, this was one of the most comprehensive and remarkable exhibits on this theme ever assembled.

*Roose-Evans, James. 1970. (136)

This compelling display aroused the onlooker to ponder such questions as "Why masks?" "What do they tell us about human-kind?" Historians and cultural anthropologists mention two dominant needs the mask fulfilled in ancient tribes. The first was protection. In ancient times, masks were part of a process of negotiation with the gods to entreat relief from famine, illness, and the threat of enemies. In other words, it was a needed insurance to achieve survival. Art historian John W. Nunley writes:

The mask provided security in an uncertain world. It allowed for human emotion to be displayed and negotiated in times of joy and stress. Its strength has been renewal itself. [*]

The Shaman healer usually wore a mask which demonstrated his willingness to enter the world of the gods. He never pretended to *be* a god, which would have been presumptuous, but the mask indicated that he was willing to approach the *realm* of the gods.

In ancient Greece, the patron god, Dionysus, presided over the coming of spring, a time of revelry and resurrection which Western cultures recognize as a time of renewal. To many this is the time of the Easter season. Theatre festivals which took place in large amphitheaters celebrated a transition from the bleakness of winter to a time of hope and abundance. In the Sophoclean tragedy *Oedipus Rex,* the Theban community gets a fresh start in life through the harrowing exploits of Oedipus.

Comedy celebrated the return of fertility in a far different style, often accompanied by grotesque masks supporting lewd and explicit sexual behavior. These masks were derived from the ancient Roman Comedy which was to be the forerunner of the comic style known as the Italian Comedy, or the Commedia dell'arte.

---

*Nunley, John W., *Masks, Faces of Culture.* Harry N. Abrams, Inc. Publishers, N.Y., 2002: p. 38.

The *Commedia* originated in 16th Century Tuscany in northern Italy. This satirical and irreverent theatre mocked the conventions of every aspect of bourgeois respectability in sight, including greed, medical practice, academia, love, marriage, hypocrisy in high places, and—when it could get away with it—religion itself. *Commedia* troupes were often at risk when the darts of mockery struck too close to home. There are accounts of outraged eruptions by the invading Spanish soldiers, then occupying the south, in witnessing themselves lampooned through the character of the outwardly swaggering but inwardly cowardly villain, Capitano. Faculties of universities were equally scandalized when the stuffy character of *il Dottore*, the tediously-moralizing and Latin-speaking doctor of letters, gabbled on interminably as everyone on stage fell asleep.

Each region produced its own object of mockery. Arlecchino, perhaps the most famous of the *Commedia* cast of characters, originated in Bergamo where this mischievous shepherd pranced over the mountainsides, desperately attempting to keep his balance. This struggle for equilibrium was a metaphor for his outrageously duplicitous behavior in chasing women, food, and money. Pantalone was the easily recognized Venetian money grubber and lecher who became the protagonist in Molière's *The Miser*. Smeraldina was often his harridan wife berating him for his flirtatiousness, even while seeking her own romantic diversions; romantic love was given a thoroughly ludicrous send-up through the character types known as the "innamorati," or fickle Neapolitan lovers, who were falling in and out of love at a rate that would outdo today's Hollywood tabloids.

This liberated style of playing was like fresh air to a populace bored stiff with the church-sponsored religious drama of the time. Consequently, *Commedia* troupes were soon in great demand all over 17th Century Europe, and the *Commedia* form was to influence western comedy for the next three centuries. World playwrights such as Molière and Marivaux, have freely adapted

Commedia styles into their plays and its influence has been felt in playwriting, opera and ballet to this day. *Commedia* is literally the father of all modern comedy.[*]

Commedia originated in the market places of Tuscany, as masked actors performed on the back of carts competing with vendors, hawkers of patent medicines and milling crowds for the attention of the audience. The Italian actors were also masters of improvisation. They knew in advance the form of a given scene, but the action was never the same. This delighted the public, as no one, including the performers, knew what would happen next!

Pierre Duchartre, perhaps the greatest authority on *Commedia* practice, records the observations of the legendary actor and theatre historian of the time, Riccoboni:

> *Impromptu comedy throws the whole weight of the performance on the acting, with the result that the same scenario may be treated in various ways and seem to be a different play each time. The actor who improvises plays in a much livelier and more natural manner than one who learns his role by heart. People feel better, and therefore say better, what they invent than what they borrow from others with the aid of memory.*[**]

---

[*]Shakespeare frequently imported Commedia "types" directly into his own plays. Consider *The Taming of the Shrew*. Petruchio is the embodiment of the Commedia's swaggering Capitano; Hortensio, the money-grubbing Pantalone; Tranio, the scheming trickster, Arlecchino; Bianca and Lucentio, the swooning lovers from the Commedia "innamorati" tradition, and so on. The influence of Commedia is also readily observable in modern pieces. In Thornton Wilder's *The Matchmaker*, the miserly Horace Vandergelder is derived from the money-pinching and lecherous Pantalone; Dolly Levi is a scheming Smeraldina (derived from the sly and fortune-telling "Strega" tradition); Barnaby echoes the nimble-footed Arlecchino; Cornelius, Ambrose, and Ermingarde are descendants of the Commedia lovers, or "innamorati." The riotous Harmony Gardens Restaurant scene is directly derived from Goldoni's *The Servant of Two Masters*.
[**]Duchartre: 1966 (32)

194

Mask performance also called for a high level of physical and verbal expressiveness, and this fact signals the importance of mask training to the contemporary actor. Pierre Duchartre, writes:

Nonus of Panopolis said of the mimes ot Theodosius' time that "they had gestures that speak a language, hands that have a mouth, fingers that have voices."

Mask training has also been found to possess an enormous potential in healing work. Noted British educator Peter Slade, now acknowledged as the "Father of Dramatherapy," spoke in 1994 on on its relevance to healing:

Masks are useful for all sorts of confidence building. I have used them for "equalizing" of status in factory groups, for patients who have had bad facial injuries, and I am now recommending them to help people from abroad who cannot yet speak English. Behind a mask, you often feel braver. The part of you which finds difficulty in facing the world is a small you. The You which grows behind a mask is a great big one.[*]

Mitch Mitchelson, an instructor of mask technique at Rose Bruford Drama College also comments on the transforming potential of mask work:

I have seen the use of commedia masks transform people's body imagery, bringing a degree of definition and vigor that were not there before the mask was used. I have seen women working with the "Strega mask"[**] draw upon an incredible power, strength, and presence in their exploration of this archetypal mask.[***]

[*] Slade, *Experience*, 125.
[**] A sinister seer/witch who traffics in love potions and advice to the lovelorn.
[***] Mitchelson, Mitch. 1996: (131)

Jocelynne James, a current director of *Sesame* at the London Central School of Speech and Drama, which specializes in healing work with adults as well as with young people writes:

One man I worked with had no voice at all when I first met him. In my exercises of this nature he seemed unable to produce sounds of any kind. It was during a dramatic enactment in which he played the role of a dragon that he first discovered his voice. Whilst using his arms and hands in a gestural display to demonstrate fire-breathing, out from his mouth emerged a penetrating noise that stopped us all in our tracks. This was a very surprising and extraordinary moment for everyone involved. It was the embodiment of the image of the dragon that empowered his voice, which continues to grow in volume and definition to this day. [*]

I interviewed Linda Cook, a veteran teacher in the New Orleans school system, at the 1997 conference of the Association for Theatre in Higher Education. Linda employs mask techniques in her primary grade classroom, and spoke to me of one of her students.

Randall did not speak for five months, and in the files was totally written off. Then one day he chose to play a monkey. His classmates were astounded as he went deeply "into role" and gave birth to sounds never heard from him before in playing this jungle creature. This was just the mental tool that Randall needed for him to get in touch with his feelings. Some weeks later he was speaking normally, rejoined the class and eventually became a leading student. [**]

* James, Jocelynne: *Ibid.* (213)
**Interview with Linda Cook, New York, June 3, 1997.

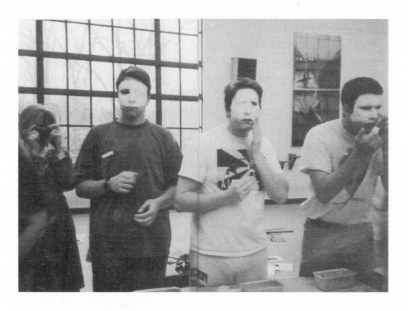

(Plate 9) Mask workshop: Principia College, 1997. (Photo courtesy of Principia College Archives)

For many years I have enjoyed performing in masks in my various mime shows in America and abroad. These performances included a series called "Gargolyles," based upon the grotesque character types, "Rumor," and "Suspicion," that have looked down upon us through the ages from the towering ramparts of Notre Dame and also masks based upon the cartoons of Honoré Daumier from his series, "La Loi et La Justice," or "Law and Justice." To acquire authenticity for the Daumier pieces, I visited the Paris law courts at the Palais de Justice. There I watched in awe as two opposing lawyers tore "a passion to tatters." Daumier got it right!

At Principia College in 1997, I conducted a performance mask workshop over a ten-week period supporting a production titled, *The Masks We Wear*. I had the good fortune to meet mask expert Hilary Chandler at a St. Louis performance of *The Bread and Puppet Theatre*, and she agreed to instruct our class in the art of mask making. Under the guidance of this skilled professional, the students created superbly expressive masks to illustrate the characters in their various pieces. (Plate 9)* The students avidly took to this adventure, working with plasticene, clay, newspaper, petroleum jelly, papier maché and plaster gauze. Touching up their creations through the application of gesso and colorful acrylics, the class was transformed into an exciting mask workshop, with Hilary's talent and expertise providing us with lifetime skills.

Witnessing our show, *The Masks We Wear,* the college community was enthralled by mask performance, which had been hitherto unknown to them. One audience member approached me afterwards, exclaiming, "I never knew this sort of thing *existed*!" And another, "Why can't we see *more* of this?!" ("Hear! Hear!")

In the spring of 1994 in Alton, Illinois, I discovered how enthusiastically children take to mask theatre when I was invited by Bonnisue Wadley to join a children's mask workshop called "*The Creative Express.*" There, delighted children of 11 to 15 years reveled in the discovery of this dynamic art form. It recalled a kind of Hallowe'en for them, where they could fantasize in becoming whatever character they wished. On the performance day, proud parents observed as a king, a princess, witches, assorted monsters, and even a *cow* made their ways to the stage!

Mask-making is a technique that any theatre teacher can acquire and impart to students. One can consult the Internet to locate experts such as Hilary Chandler. There are also books on mask-making at major bookstores. Some of these contain instructions on the creation of masks from the simplest material, such as cardboard or paper. The process requires little financial outlay,

*For an excerpt from this show, see the chapter on *Masks,* in the two-part video version of this book.

and the rewards are great. Satisfying and joyous moments of bonding with the community transpire, as parents, teachers and friends support the children performing their original works.

I close this section with a story that illustrates what mask performance can achieve in the classroom. It took place in a 1992 Period Styles acting class at Principia College.

Laure Anne's Moment of Glory

For the first six weeks in our Period Styles acting class at Principia College, Laure Anne spoke so quietly we had to strain to hear her. Members of the class could be observed bending forward when she spoke, and on her best days, she might be heard in the second row. This is a typical plight with many college student actors today, as they have so little background in speaking with proper voice support.

Each student actor in the class was asked to create a scene based on the shenanigans that they had studied in *Commedia* scenarios. They were then to improvise on these scenes in authentic *Commedia* masks and slapsticks, which were provided for their use.

On this particular day, modest Laure Anne had chosen to play—of all things—the fiery servant girl, Smeraldina, opposite her womanizing lover, Arlecchino. Now if ever there could have been an actor chosen by a perversely mischievous casting god to take on this tempestuously jealous Xantippe, modest Laure Anne would have had to be the prime candidate!

The scene was announced:

It is 5 A.M. and Smeraldina is furious about the chronic infidelity of Arlecchino, who has been "fooling around" all night. Laure Anne, behind the mask of Smeraldina, is about to enter.

"Shhh. Here she comes!" whispers someone in the class. One

199

could sense the class musing, "How on *earth* will our demure Laure Ann handle *this* one?"

Confronting the audience, Smeraldina arrives at center stage and delivers an explanatory opening monologue, a convention of *Commedia* performance designed to inform the audience of the character's problem. Smeraldina confides to us:

"Oh, if you only knew how angry I am! That Arlecchino betrays me every night with another. Last night it was Cintia. Look! Her scarf that he dropped on the Rialto, and my friend picked it up. Ooohhhh! Just WAIT until I get my hands on him! Ooooooh!"

The distant tones of fury. ("Not *bad,* Laure Anne.")

Smeraldina suddenly observes Arlecchino approaching, and hides in the background, a vengeful cat awaiting the appearance of her lecherous mouse.

The capricious Arlecchino dances merrily onto the scene, oblivious of the smoldering Smeraldina hidden behind an imaginary tree. He delivers his own monologue describing his red-hot nocturnal escapade, complete with appropriate pelvic gyrations. Smeraldina, piqued by this demonstration of explicit erotica, can no longer contain herself. The infuriated cat springs from her hiding place! The class leans forward as if anticipating a triple axle from a neophyte skater.

The two now face each other in a primal confrontation; Laure-Anne's body actually *resembles* a hissing cat!

"You!" Smeraldina exclaims.

"Well, hel—hel—hello there, Smeraldina!" from the red-handed Arlecchino.

"HELLO?!" Laure Anne exclaims, emotion rising. "HELLO? HELLO?!!" and suddenly Laure Anne's rising voice comes from some subterranean place.

"Yes, Smeraldina . . . You know I was just looking for you . . . I . . . I . . .

"You <u>what</u>?"

"I . . . I . . . ay—yay—yay—yay-yi! . . . I . . ."

"You WHAT?!" (cutting him off, an action that Laure Anne would never permit herself in real life. Now advancing toward him): "You WHAT? You WHAT? You WHAT?!!"

"Well, last night . . . uh . . . I . . . I . . . I was on my way home, and . . . I . . . turned the corner . . . uh . . . and . . . I turned the corner . . . I turned the corner . . . and there was this . . . this PIRATE! . . ."

"OH YEAH!"

"Yes, and . . . and he had a big sword . . . I mean BIG . . . like this . . . he . . . he . . ."

"He *what?*"

"He . . . he . . . hee-hee-hee-hee" . . .

"He *what?* DON'T GIVE ME THAT!!"

The class spontaneously breaks out into applause and cheers of delight. Laure Anne is going wild! Encouraged by her public, Laure Anne now *really* takes off, building the rhythm.

"What's THIS?" she demands, brandishing the incriminating pink scarf.

"This? . . . Oh . . . oh, this?"

"Yes THIS!" waving it tauntingly in front of him. "THIS YOU LIAR!" (slapping him with it.) "THIS! THIS! THIS!" (chasing him in a circle.)

"Wait, I can explain . . ."

"You can explain nothing, nothing, NOTHING, YOU LIAR!" (She grabs his "slapstick," a *Commedia* prop designed to land a blow with a loud clatter but with no real damage. She sets about beating Arlecchino across the thighs and buttocks.)

WHACK! . . . "OUCH." . . .

WHACK! "WAIT."

Whack! Whack!

"NO, NO, PLEASE!"

"YES!" Whack!

"NO!" Whack!

"YES! YES! YES!" WHACK! WHACK! WHACK! WHACK!

The couple engage in a mad chase and eventually tumble helter-skelter into the wings where the whacking *continues!* The class roars and screams its approval for some moments before the startled Laure Ann reappears. The applause greeting her performance is deafening. Some of the class were quaking and brushing away tears.

What a triumph to cherish for all time!

Encountering our "Smeraldina" once more on a recent performance tour in Milan only served to confirm this transformation. Laure Anne has grown in confidence, and now speaks with a developed authority.

O, ancient buskers, we thank thee for the gift of the mask!

ELEVEN

HUMOR AND CLOWNING
(DVD disc 2: section 3)

On the morning of January 31st of 1998, Barry Bittman, M.D., was delivering the keynote address at the 10th Anniversary conference of the American Association for Therapeutic Humor in Washington, D.C. before an audience of over 400. Above him, to the audience's left, towered a large screen where Dr. Bittman would illustrate his points. The audience consisted of some 400 M.D.s, therapists, registered nurses, and other members of the medical profession interested in the healing powers of laughter.

In his role as keynote speaker, Dr. Bittman was helping us to understand the physiological process by which humor heals. World respected psychoneuroimmunologist (thank you) Bittman was describing, by way of a striking power-point visual accompaniment, how laughter is such a powerful healing agent in the healing process.

The lights were turned down. The atmosphere turned dramatic. Here was this vast army of white cells, indicated by Bittner's pointer, moving freely over the battlefields and dominating the hapless victim's bloodstream. In an intimidated corner, the outnumbered red corpuscles, representing the Army of Health, cowered in a cluster, contemplating an attack from the menacing Whites. It looked bad for the Reds.

But suddenly the distant sound of a giggle was heard as the slumbering Reds now stirred and showed signs of life. Giggles evolving into laughter served to produce more Reds. As hearty laughter reached an apex, the evil Whites are ignominiously chased from the "champs de bataille," and the day goes to the jubi-lantly victorious Reds!

I was the only actor and non-medical attendee at the conference, and the only thing I could think about was Laurence Olivier at the Battle of Agincourt in the film, *Henry V*. The graphic depiction of the effect of escalating laughter was as if Olivier were shouting, "Once more into the breach, dear 'corpuscles', once more . . ." and to the lamenting Westmoreland, hoping for a larger army, "Wish not one corpuscle more!"

This account of the Red victory may seem too playfully simplistic to be true. But Bittman was hardly announcing a career change to stand-up comedy. Dr. Bittman is a distinguished member of the medical profession, and holds the title of Medical Director of the Mind-Body Wellness Center in Meadville, Pennsylvania. He is also a highly respected neurologist, author, international speaker and inventor. Bittman's credentials are not the point here, however, but rather his activity in providing members of the medical profession with serious information on how laughter heals.

Proofs of the healing power of laughter date from the 1970's discovery of Norman Cousins, former editor of the *Saturday Review of Literature*. Cousins stunned the medical profession in recovering from an illness that had been pronounced terminal by several medical authorities. For those not acquainted with his story, here is a summary.

Cousins was dispatched by the U.S. government on a Moscow peace-keeping mission during the "Cold War." Returning to the United States and feeling his ambassadorial work a complete failure, Cousins' mental stress led to a troubling illness. Ultimately, reputable members of the medical profession diagnosed his case and gave him no hope for survival. His story is detailed in his book, *Anatomy of an Illness: Reflections on Healing and Regeneration.*

Having nothing to lose, Cousins decided to take responsibility for his own healing. He informed his doctor, Dr. Hertzig, that he wished to laugh for a few minutes each day and embarked on a regular daily laughter program. Sensing the atmosphere of the hospital inimical to his experiment, he was granted a hotel room where he could laugh for longer periods without embarrassment. Cousins then requested a series of videotapes of old films of the Marx Brothers, Laurel and Hardy and The Three Stooges, as well as a series of *Candid Camera* replays. With these, he would sustain longer periods of laughter in his private room.

The results are well-known. After persisting with the humor program for some weeks, Cousins achieved a complete recovery validated by reports of reputable doctors. *The Medical Journal* published official news of the story, and in 1979 Cousins described the account in his book, *The Anatomy of an Illness as Perceived by the Patient: Reflections on Healing and Regeneration.* Soon he was inundated with mail from all corners of the world seeking to understand how his healing was accomplished.

At the heart of Cousins' experiment was an insight he shared in his book:

> *The inevitable question arose in my mind: what about the positive emotions? If negative emotions produce negative chemical changes in the body, wouldn't the positive emotions produce positive chemical changes? Is it possible that love hope, faith, laughter, confidence and the will to live have therapeutic value? Do chemical changes occur only on the* <u>downside?</u>[*]

The medical profession now generally concedes that laughter is capable of altering the chemistry of the body sufficiently to contribute to the restoration of health. "Laughter groups" are springing up all over the world. An example is the Gesundheit! Center of

*Cousins, *Anatomy*, 14, 15.

Patch Adams, M.D., where non-medical care and laughter have produced thousands of healing transformations since its inception. As an extension of his theories, Adams has been leading "healing through humor" clown tours through the trouble spots of the world.

Author-journalist and TV host Bill Moyers has published a volume, *Healing and the Mind,* which also examines how a change of thought leads to healing. The book records statements from many reputable members of the medical profession including Thomas Delbanco of Beth Israel Hospital in Boston, whom Moyers interviewed:

> *Moyers: Watching you with your patients, I get the sense that you treat the body and appeal to the mind. Is that a fair characterization?*

> *Delbanco: I hope I'm addressing both the body and the mind. But they're so intertwined that it's hard for me to differentiate. I know more about the body than the mind. It's probably the easier to study and that's what we learned in medical school—ninety-five percent body and five percent mind. But I'll tell you, once you're in practice, and you're taking care of real people, it becomes much closer to fifty-fifty.*

In a later segment of the interview Delbanco states:

> *Mind and body are inextricably woven together. Every primary physician knows that . . . We'd better be educated in both if we're going to serve those patients well.*

The research of Dean Ornish, M.D. is highly respected. This eminent physician holds many titles including Assistant Clinical

*Moyers, *Healing,* 7, 8.

Professor of Medicine and President and Director of the Preventive Medicine Research Institute at the School of Medicine, University of California, San Francisco. Ornish states in an extended colloquy with Moyers:

> *There is a real yearning for community in our culture. I think that is one of the reasons you see so many different types of support groups, such as AA, Overeaters Anonymous, or our cardiac support group. It's too bad that in our culture you often have to have an illness or an addiction before you can become part of a community. . . . Well, we're learning. A number of studies have shown* that people who feel isolated have three to five times the mortality, not only from cardiovascular disease, but from all causes, when compared to people who don't feel isolated.[*]

Many of society's troubled children also suffer from feelings of isolation, which in turn can lead to all kinds of social disorders. If we accept the Ornish premise that social alienation contributes to *physical* illness, we can identify many problems with which so many of our young people struggle.

Norman Cousins attributed his healing to the introduction of *opposite* qualities to those which had produced his illness. He had reached a low point of a depression caused by a lack of self-worth. In his view of things, he had let down millions of his countrymen, and this overwhelming guilt led to a deep state of depression and then to his illness.

His healing process involved a process of reversal. Stress was ultimately put to flight through the introduction of opposite qualities to those which had caused the stress.

It is important to note that in his book, Cousins does not limit healing to laughter. His larger point is the need for a transformed

*Ibid., 87.

mental outlook. We cite a statement from his *Anatomy of an Illness*:

> *Increasingly, in the medical press, articles are being published about the high cost of the negative emotions. Cancer, in particular, has been connected to intensive states of grief or anger or fear. It makes little sense to suppose that emotions exact only penalties and confer no benefits. At any rate, long before my own serious illness, I became convinced that creativity, the will to live, hope, faith and love have biochemical significance and contribute strongly to healing and to well-being. The positive emotions are life-giving experiences.* [*]

Our studies with teenagers cited in the early chapters of this book, clearly point to Cousins' principle at work. Theatre provided these kids with programs which kindled, in the words of Cousins, "the will to live, hope, faith and love." And these programs saved them.

Many of the difficulties our children and teenagers encounter, as we have seen in this book, have been caused by alienation and destructive labeling. These thought currents, once taken into the *mental* "bloodstream" lead to feelings of inadequacy, alienation, and hopelessness. At this moment the healing theatre arrives with other information: "You are *not* alone; you are *not* inadequate, and you cannot be *labeled* thus. You are with us and we are with you as part of a connected and loving family."

Our society is a 'body" which has permitted the "wrong corpuscles," to run unchecked and rampant in poisoning our children. Here is where Norman Cousins' question is so apt: "If negative emotions produce negative chemical changes in the body, wouldn't the positive emotions produce positive chemical changes?"

*Ibid., 86.

Where theatre activity is promoting health among our young, we see these "red corpuscle" qualities of inclusion and bonding at work, counteracting the poisonous social influences of labeling, limitation and separation.

To paraphrase Cousins, we might say, "If society's negative atmosphere of alienation, hopelessness and violence is poisoning our children, let us provide them with the health-giving counter-forces of inclusion, connection, and celebration."

Bringing Laughter to the Classroom and the World

One reason many teachers are reluctant to utilize humor in the classroom comes from a limited concept of humor. To many, the mention of humor will suggest exaggerated behavior, or what stand-up comedians or clowns do. Certainly few are born to these professions, and comparing ourselves with another's expression of humor is a barrier to finding our own.

I was intrigued to meet registered nurse Patty Wooten, BSN, at the 1998 Washington, D.C. conference of the American Association of Therapeutic Humor. She has done superb healing work in hospitals with her puppet, Shobi Dobi, and passes these techniques on to others through her "Hospital Clown Newsletter—Heart to Heart Caring Clowns," and through her book, *Compassionate Laughter*. In an interview in *The Journal of Nursing Jocularity*, she was once asked: "How would you describe your clown?" Her answer was, "Well, I'm really more fun than funny." This is an interesting response that many of us who are tentative about humor might consider. I feel that self-made clown, Wooten, seems to be sharing a meaningful discovery which we might paraphrase: "The kingdom of 'Clowndom' is *within* you," or the comic spirit is there, we are born with it, but must now coax it into action. Asked in the interview "How can people get in touch with this clown?" Wooten corroborated this theory:

If you can begin to laugh at yourself, then you will open up the bubble of joy inside of you. I never pass a mirror without making a silly face. Some people, like me, have a very rubber-like face, able to create countless expressions. I wasn't born with that rubber face. I acquired it through use! I suggest you stand in front of a mirror and make faces until you start to laugh. [*]

There are now thousands of laughter groups worldwide. A special feature account of these groups appearing in the June 9, 2004 *Christian Science Monitor*, reports on some of their leaders. Robyn Sadler is one of about 1,000 adults in the United States, Canada, and Mexico who have become certified laughter leaders through the *World Laughter Tour, Inc.* [**] The group was formed in 1998 by former psychologist and psychotherapist Steve Wilson and nurse Karen Buxman. Their intent is global influence in the practical applications of laughter and humor for health and world peace. Mr. Wilson, a self-proclaimed "joyologist" states:

"If everyone would go back to being a child again by spending 30 minutes laughing, the whole world would be a better place. [***]

Today there are a wide number of clown troupes that can prove helpful in developing humor skills. The St. Louis-based Association of Therapeutic Humor is one. This organization holds annual conferences including laughter workshops applicable to virtually every human setting. The year I attended in 1999 there were workshops applying laughter to the corporate meeting, to the classroom, to the political conference, and even in hospitals where patients were struggling with judgments of terminal illnesses. I

*Wooten, Patty, BSN, *Journal of Nursing Jocularity.* Vol. 8. No. 1. (58)
**Web address: www.laughtertour.com
***Fritscher-Porter, Karen: *Christian Science Monitor.* ed. June 9, 2004. (18)

found the techniques of clowning so accessible that I could readily share them with my college students. I have kept in touch with some of these laughter therapists along the way who utilize these techniques in their professions as therapists, educators, entertainers, preachers and doctors.

Nothing could have reinforced the theory of Patty Wooten, that "we all have a clown within us" more indelibly than when I was invited to join an international 2002 "Healing through Humor Clown Tour, " sponsored by world famous and international clown and healer, Patch Adams.

In the late 60's Patch Adams, M.D., found the atmosphere of the hospital sadly lacking in providing hope. Turning from a conventionally developed medical practice, he founded Gesundheit! University in West Arlington, Virginia. Health care at Gesundheit! consisted of imparting joy, hope and compassion, with humor as the main ingredient. Thousands passed through its doors to emerge healed and rejuvenated. Adams has written a seminal book on the subject, *Gesundheit!* In it he cites Dr. Thomas Sydenhan, a physician of the 17th Century:

The arrival of a good clown exercises more beneficial influence upon the health of a town than of twenty laden with drugs.

Adams never denigrates those who seek whatever means of healing they wish to follow, and never wants his findings to be taken as a religion.

We must not make our techniques a religion that we follow even when they don't help. We are healers; caring, empathetic, thoughtful friends to our patients. Our magic is not in our tools but in ourselves. If a treatment helps, does it matter why? . . . There

(Plate 10) The Patch Adams Trans-Siberian Healing Through Humor Troupe at the Lyuverna Rehab Center for Children in Ekaterinburg, Siberia, August 5, 2003.

are great healers in all phases of health care. If all these systems worked together, a patient's care could be entrusted to an active partnership. This would be beneficial for the allopath, the alternative healer, and the patient.[*]

*Adams, Patch, M.D., *Gesundheit!* 1993. (55)

(Plate 11) Clown visit to the prison for "Young Offenders," Ulan Ude, Siberia, 2003. (Photo courtesy of Trey Cromwell)

(Plate 12) "Today everyone becomes a clown!" Face painting: Central Children's Clinic and Hospital, Irkutsk, Siberia, 2003. (Photo courtesy of Bill Waters)

(Plate 13) "Das vedanya!" A heartfelt and reluctant "goodbye."
The Zagorsky Family and Children's House Orphanage, Ulan
Ude, Siberia, 2003. (Photo courtesy of Bill Waters)

Patch has sponsored *Healing Through Humor Clown Tours* in all the trouble spots of the world for many years, and I was fortunate to be included in one of them. Our particular voyage carried us the length of Russia, from Moscow to Vladivostock, a distance of 5000 miles covering six time zones. We were fourteen "clowns" whose purpose was to bring joy and laughter to hospitals, orphanages, prisons, and a home for the elderly. (Plate 10) We ended up clowning at three and sometimes four facilities a day. These included many orphanages, hospitals, often for children deemed with little hope of recovery, prisons for "young offenders,"—a deeply moving experience—and a home for the elderly where we danced with beautiful elderly citizens to the creaking strains of an ancient accordion, lovingly squeezed out by the gnarled hands of a darling babushka! (Plates 11, 12, and 13)

214

In pursuing Patty Wooten's theory that we all have this clown within us, very few had ever "clowned" in public, and, but for our zany home-made costumes, makeup, and red noses, we hardly considered ourselves clowns. There was a therapist, a young doctor, a college student, a magician, an experienced preacher, teachers, a social worker and so forth. So we were 14 complete strangers to each other and from diverse occupations hardly connected with clowning. But that is what Patch Adams has done for years—insisted that if the willingness is there, so also is the talent to support it. As we took off from Newark Airport in August, 2002, I must admit to feelings of doubt as to how things would pan out. We lugged weighty sacks crammed with toys, musical instruments, children's clothing, balloons, stickers, bubble-blowers, CD players, coloring books, face paints, crayons and everything else we could think of that might delight the many gatherings of Russian children we were about to encounter.

The realization that we were bonded "cheek by jowl" in this experience soon created feelings of great unity. During our performances, nobody ever interfered with another's "act," and there was never a whine or a whimper, even on long days and nights of an often torrid Siberian summer. Conditions which challenged endurance evoked great generosity. One female clown included in her luggage a folding wheelchair, transported all the way from Oregon as a gift for a hospitalized Russian girl afflicted with cerebral palsy, encountered on a clown trip the previous year. Their reunion—which was recorded on a video camera—was one of the most deeply moving moments of our tour.

Our tour guide, a beautiful and encouraging Muscovite, Olga Boyarskaya, would apprise us of how we were doing along the way. After each performance she would announce on the bus loudspeaker encouraging words of gratitude:

Dear Clowns. You made the children so happy! The director of the hospital said the children didn't want you ever to leave. They only

(Plate 14) Mime workshop for "inner city" children of Milan, Italy, April, 1997. (Photo courtesy of Bente Morse)

want you to come back again. Thank you, dear Clowns, "Spacebo!" ("Thank you"), Thank you! (see plates of Siberian children).

The entire tour was a demonstration of those feelings expressed by Nurse-Clown Patty Wooten: that in a remote and shady corner within each of us, there is a neglected clown awaiting but the permission to dance into the light.

Performing in more than twenty-five countries has shown me the remarkable potential of theatre to touch the hearts of audiences in all corners of the world. Sharing of one's art also invariably leads to *moving and unforgettable encounters.* (Plates 14 and 15)

In the final days of our Healing Through Humor Siberian Tour, we visited Tarbagatay Village, near Ulan Ude (pronounced Ooh-lan' Ooh-day). All at once, the bus stopped and we were requested to disembark to climb a hill in order to appreciate a breath-

216

(Plate 15) Harare International Festival of the Arts, Harare, Zimbabwe, May, 1998. (Photo courtesy of Bente Morse)

217

taking view of the valley below. After some twenty minutes the going got steep, and we were obliged to leverage ourselves slowly upward by gripping exposed roots and rocks. This arduous climb finally got us to the summit. We were now breathing heavily, but the view of the vast golden valley below was magnificent and well worth the effort.

The climb that we were requested to make was to serve a larger purpose. As we sprawled breathlessly on the soft Siberian turf, eight magnificently costumed men and women suddenly appeared from behind the cover of a great rock. We gasped in disbelief. Was this a newly discovered apparition of Boris Godunov? Or a Siberian production of *Lost Horizon Revisited*? Olga, our guide, whispered, "Old Believers," referring to a sect that had immigrated to the region a century earlier in fleeing the persecution of the czars.

With no visible cue, eight magnificent voices filled the air with a rousing anthem of welcome that boomeranged through the entire valley, stirring every fiber of our beings. We sat transfixed.

That evening, with our feet once more on earth, the magnificent celebration continued at a local tavern. We were treated to a meal of delicious cabbage soup, stuffed dumplings and a flavorful salad. The dinner was followed by games, a simulated wedding of two of our highly attractive young "clowns," in which richly designed costumes were provided by our hosts for the occasion, and an exchange of songs and dancing into the night. (Plate 16)

How could one ever forget such an evening? Art had provided a magical trampoline on which we were all children bounding and rebounding higher and higher in an exhilarating dance to human fellowship.

(Plate 16) Our generous hosts, "The Old Believers," provide a moving and memorable farewell to Ulan Ude. (Photo courtesy of Bill Waters)

TWELVE

PRISONS AND THE POWER OF ART

"The blatant truth is that art needs to be in the school curriculum. Some sort of cultural tie-in has to be there for all youth. Otherwise they're just going to become alienated and they're going to turn on society. That just seems so obvious. And yet you don't see school boards and probation departments making that connection."
—Grady Hillman, interview in *Art in the Public Interest*, 1996

In 1974 I attended a New York Public Theater production of Miguel Piñero's play, *Short Eyes*, at Lincoln Center. The work was based upon his own prison experiences and those of the troupe, who had all met in an upstate Bedford Hills, New York, prison and called themselves, "The Family."

Marvin Felix Camillo, the director of the play, was an actor in residence in Sing Sing prison when he met Piñero in 1972. Camillo began to direct a group of prisoners in a series of plays, and one show, *Prison Sounds* caught the eye of *New York Times* theater critic, Mel Gussow, who wrote favorably about the play. Camillo writes in describing the event:

> *The warden at Sing Sing read Gussow's article, called us into his office, and read us the Riot Act. He called it contraband. I called it good poetry.*[*]

*Camillo, Marvin Felix. 1974. "Introduction" (viii) 1974.

Camillo describes the history of the group leading to the 1974 Lincoln Center production:

I met men as they were released and brought them from a prison slave system to a Manhattan workshop that they themselves created; and so they could avoid the cold, hard existence that had faced them so many times before. Instead of going back to the block or a kind of situation that could lead them back to jail, they went to a workshop to rehearse. Work was the operative word. We met and worked and worked until everybody was exhausted. Often there was no money for food or carfare, but somehow we managed to scrape up something for the night or the next day's rehearsal. Work was beginning to take on real meaning. Commitment was heavy. We were working in the Players' Workshop on the Lower East Side, which the actors had been known to walk to from as far away as Harlem. My studio apartment in Manhattan served as a refuge for whoever needed it. At some point every member of The Family had taken me up on my invitation: "Esta es tu casa." ("This is your home.") [*]

The *Short Eyes* cast formed and began rehearsing the play in New York City and remained somehow cohesive through all kinds of economic and other challenges until actress Colleen Dewhurst brought the play to the attention of Joe Papp, founder and director New York's Public Theater, who produced the play at Lincoln Center.

The play involves the brutal gang murder of a prisoner, which all the inmates, along with the complicit prison authorities, succeed in having labeled a "suicide." *Short Eyes* represents a scathing indictment of the United States correctional system, revealing practices of unsupervised violence, torture and murder. It must

*Ibid., xiii.

have surely raised the question on the part of its audiences, "How in a civilized nation could these wretched conditions possibly exist?"

But similar events have been abundantly documented in reports sponsored by Human Rights Watch, The Department of Justice and Amnesty International, indicating that Piñero's account is no exaggeration.

The incentive to keep our prisons full has been for some years a tactical political strategy as author Brent Staples comments in an op-ed article in the December 27th issue of *The New York Times*:

> *The New York Republican Party uses its majority in the State Senate to maintain political power, through fat years and lean. The Senate Republicans, in turn, rely on their large upstate delegation to keep that majority. Whether those legislators have consciously made the connection or not, it's hard to escape the fact that bulging prisons are good for their districts. The advantages extend beyond jobs and political gerrymandering. By counting unemployed inmates as residents, the prison counties lower their per capita incomes—and increase the portion they get of federal funds for the poor. This results in a transfer of federal cash from places that can't afford to lose it to places that don't deserve it.* [*]

Alan Elsner has written extensively on the American prison system, and is the author of a 2004 book, *Gates of Injustice*. In this volume, Elsner details two notable themes: the inhuman cruelty that transpires within our incarceration facilities, and the rampant dishonesty and greed of administrators and public officials who profit from it. A full mention of abuses found in our prisons lies beyond the scope of this book, but here is one extract from Elsner's volume:

*Staples, Brent. *New York Times,* Dec. 27, 2004. (A2)

Numbers tell us nothing about the sheer brutality of life for many thousands of people in U.S. prisons and jails. Statistics alone cannot do justice to the widespread abuses and violations of human rights that pervade the prison system from top to bottom. It is a system in which hundreds of thousands of men are raped each year; in which racist and neo-Nazi gangs run drugs, gambling and prostitution rings from inside their prison cells, buying and selling weak and vulnerable fellow inmates as sex slaves, while the authorities turn a blind eye. It is a system in which thousands of inmates are subjected to virtual sensory deprivation and social isolation for years on end and often driven crazy, if they were not seriously mentally ill to begin with. It is a system in which large numbers of women are sexually abused and hundreds of thousands of mentally ill individuals get little or no treatment. It is also a world in which corrections officers risk daily assaults, poor health, broken marriages and premature deaths.[*]

Reverend Jesse Jackson, quoted in this same volume, observes:

We are often tempted to think that China is an oppressive country, but we incarcerate 500,000 more people in this country—despite the fact that we have less than one-fourth the population of China. We lock up our poor, our uneducated, our unruly, our unstable and our addicted, where other countries provide treatment, mental hospitals and care.[**]

Our children and teenagers are among the most pathetic victims of this race to incarcerate. The Nelson Rockefeller drug laws passed in 1973 included an automatic fifteen-year prison term for

[*]Elsner, *Gates*, 12.
[**]Jackson, Rev. Jesse L. Sr. *Liberty and Justice for Some. Mother Jones.* July 10, 2001. As quoted in Elsner, 12.

possessing small amounts of narcotics for adults and children. Many other states followed. This meant that a sixteen-year-old first offender could spend his youth in prison for possessing a gram of marijuana.

Children and teenagers suffered in many other ways, as Elsner points out:

> *Children are some of the saddest invisible casualties of the U.S. prison binge. The BJS (Bureau of Justice Statistics) in 2000, estimated that 721,500 of America's prisoners, excluding jail inmates, were parents of at least one child, while at least 1.5 million children had a parent in prison. Children whose parents are incarcerated experience a broad range of problems, including rage, guilt, low self-esteem and depression. They are more likely to live in poverty, more likely to fail at school, more likely to take drugs and more likely to end up in juvenile jail. Half of all juveniles in custody have a parent or close relative in prison.* [*]

Thousands of teenagers have been sentenced as adults, many of whom had little awareness of what they were doing. But what is far more tragic is the story of so many young people who have found themselves on death row. They have been provided with inadequate legal protection as they were invariably poor with no chance at reform, and spent many years on death row before being executed. Here is one of their stories.

Author and historian, James Cahill, appeared on the November 27, 2007 edition of the National Public Radio program, *The Bill Moyers Journal*. Cahill recounted how he had heard of the case of Dominique Green, an event which caused Cahill to drop all involvement with his customary field of history to research and document this account for a forthcoming book.

---

*Bureau of Justice Statistics. *Almost 1.5 Million Have a Mother or Father in Prison.* Washington, August 30, 2000. As quoted in Elsner, 25.

Dominique Green was a black nineteen-year-old, when he was convicted of murder in Texas. Cahill, who got to know Green in frequent meetings, states:

He came from an alcoholic and drug-dealing household. He had been sexually abused several times, and was put in juvenile homes . . . just about everything that could be done to him that anyone could imagine being done to a child, was done to him. [*]

From the beginning, Green insisted on his innocence, but the only witness to the crime had fled and could not be reached for further questioning. He was finally granted a re-trial years later, in which his lawyer slept through the entire proceeding. The court refused to admit this circumstance as a deterrent to judgment, as there was no Constitutional law prohibiting an attorney from sleeping in a courtroom. During these years Green read omnivorously, and one volume that particularly impressed him was Archbishop Desmond Tutu's *No Future Without Forgiveness,* which led Green to spread the word of forgiveness among his fellow prisoners over a period of many years. Cahill heard the case, and eventually got the attention of Archbishop Desmond Tutu, who pleaded vehemently for a re-trial with Human Rights Watch organization in Rome. The case reached the American Supreme Court in 2004, but a re-trial was denied because the appeal was, in the court's judgment, "too late." In other words, it was too late for justice to be done. On 7:59 of October 26, 2004, Dominique Green was executed.

Poet and writer Grady Hillman has for many years witnessed the efficacy of arts programs in prisons. He became involved in the field of corrections through a 1981 creative writing residency in

* Interview with James Cahill, *Bill Moyers Journal,* National Public Radio, November 27, 2007.

225

the Texas prison system, and since then, he has worked in over 50 correctional institutions in six states and four countries. Author of two books of poetry, including a book of translations from the Quechua Inca tradition, he co-founded the Southwest Correctional Arts Network (SCAN), and currently serves as a valued consultant to many correctional and arts agencies around the nation and the world.

Hillman writes in his authoritative handbook, *Arts Programs for Juvenile Offenders in Detention and Corrections: A Guide to Promising Practices*, sponsored by the Juvenile Justice System and the National Endowment for the Arts:

> *Young people who are involved in the criminal justice system are at high risk for a myriad of ongoing behaviors. In most cases, they lack the skills, self-respect, motivation, role models and support systems that will help them become responsible adults. One type of intervention that has been demonstrated to work successfully to address and counter these challenges and to re-direct young people away from violence—no matter whether the juvenile's court involvement includes truancy, community-based sanctions, detention or juvenile correctional institutions—is participation in arts programs. Arts programs provide significant impact for a relatively small outlay of money.*

In a published 1996 interview with Steven Durland, entitled, "Maintaining Humanity," Hillman describes the effects of arts programs in the prisons:

Steven Durland: *Times are tough. How do you justify arts-in-prison programs? There's always that argument, "Why should we support these programs? This is taxpayer money and we could be spending that money on other programs. These guys in prison need to be punished.*

Gary Hillman: *But California, Oklahoma and Massachusetts have* *come with documentation that shows that when you bring an arts program into an adult correctional setting it reduces the incident rate—everything from stealing steaks from the commons area to stabbing other inmates—by sixty to ninety per cent. You can document this readily because there's a high degree of surveillance and observation. Those programs were able to really document the radical rate of personal transformation within the institution. . . . California quantified that on a cost basis and found that arts programs in prisons not only paid for themselves, but provided significant savings for the institutions at the same time. There was one study of four arts programs in the state that were funded to the tune of $125,000. Some independent professors from UC Santa Barbara were able to quantify the incident rate reduction and found that the institution actually saved $225,000 through the effects of the program.*

SD: *It sounds like what you've got is more than an argument for art in prisons, but for art in the schools.*

GH: *Yes. Definitely. Where we were looking at the Harris County juvenile probation department, I was working with these artists and they were reporting back to me. They kept saying, "These programs are great." The kids are eating it up. But why didn't they get it in school? Why didn't they have this opportunity before?" If they'd had this opportunity then they probably wouldn't have wound up in this setting . . . They had very powerful forces working in their lives and they needed something to turn to that would give them a way to get a handle on their lives. . . . In the correctional facility they start getting a handle on their lives through the arts. They have to face up to who they are, and where they've been and who the people are in their lives. The tragedies and the stories. And suddenly they transcend. They get on top of it. Had that happened in the schools, many of them wouldn't have turned out that way.*

SD: *What kind of artist does this work? What are the necessary*

227

skills? It's not the sort of thing you take a class on in school, and I'd guess that not everyone is cut out for this kind of work.

GH: *You're right. Art therapists have a role to play in society and art teachers have their role to play. But the model that I promote, the model that I think is the best, is the professional artist and the artist-mentor relationship. The master artist. When I look for an artist to come into a correctional setting, I generally look for someone who's good and has proved themselves in the free world. . . . What they want from you is to show them what you do. They want somebody who will give them feedback on what they do. They want a professional standard. They want to know how good they are. And they want to know what they need to do to get better.*

What you want is somebody who can go into a prison setting and look at them as human beings. They've made some tragic mistakes. A lot of artists want to know what they did. I don't. I never want to know what kind of crimes they committed. I don't want to be put in a position of my own moral values judging them. That's not my role. They've been judged, they've been convicted. I'm just there to share, and give them my perception and feedback and criticism so they can make adjustments in their work so their work can develop and they can become better writers.

I tend to stay away from art therapists and art teachers, because they come in with a curriculum. I don't like people to come in with a curriculum. I like people to come in with technique and experience with art. That's what works best.

I contacted Gary Hillman in January of 2003, and he granted me time to hear more of his views on the importance of art in prisons.[*]

RM: *Would you tell me what form, or forms, these workshops take?*

*Gary Hillman, telephone interview with the author, January 23, 2004.

GH: *I've worked in over a hundred correctional facilities in twenty states and four countries, using, besides writing, dance and drama.*

RM: *What kind of thing happens with these prisoners in an arts program?*

GH: *A number of things can happen, both with juvenile justice and adult prisoners. You are providing inmates an opportunity to work with those in the world, to work with the world. By this, you are enabling them to explore the world around them as well as the world inside them. The programs make the institutions look good. That's because arts programs provide a bridge to the community which otherwise wouldn't exist.*

RM: *Since this work is so effective, why wouldn't the government, or the authorities, seize upon this fact and expand these programs?*

GH: *I've seen a general decline in arts programs for adult inmates, but I've seen a large increase in arts programs for juvenile offenders. That's both good and bad. We're reaching more juveniles, so that's a positive.*

RM: *There is a big issue here with funding, right?*

GH: *If an arts organization has funding, that's good, naturally. On the other hand I've known no one that doesn't want to work because it's so transient. I think these programs are so important because the situations of the prisoners are so stressful, and even one or two arts workshops can be effective.*

RM: *What is your overall view then of the effectiveness of arts programs in the prisons?*

GH: *I do think that arts programs remain the most effective juvenile justice programs we have. Arts programs provide a bridge to the community which otherwise wouldn't exist. And once you have these programs, a lot of things can happen. You are providing inmates the opportunity to work with tools that connect them with the world. And then to realize their power which will enable them to explore this world around them as well as the world inside them.*

There are many theatre programs available to help inmates move forward upon their re-entrance into the outside world. One such group is called "Shakespeare Behind Bars," a program at the Luther Luckett Correctional Complex in LaGrange, Kentucky. The program is directed by three volunteers, Curt Tofteland, Director of the prison, Larry Chandler, warden, and Karen Heath, staff sponsor. For the main part, activity focuses on producing the plays of Shakespeare. Costumes may be fabricated of sheets, with strips of cloth for headbands; props include light wooden swords.

An extensive 2004 *Christian Science Monitor* article describes how prisoners acquire invaluable insights into their life conditions through performing these plays. *Titus Andronicus* was presented by twenty-three inmates of this medium-security prison for their relatives and friends. Acting out the savagery of the play touched upon the issue that had caused so much pain to them and to their loved ones.

Another example involved a prisoner named Sammie, who was serving time for a violent crime. One role he played in the Lockett prison program was that of Proteus who attempts a rape at the end of *Two Gentlemen of Verona*. Sammie claims that playing that role brought back details of his crime, also involving rape, that he never understood. Two years later, Sammie chose the title role in *Othello*, where, in the final scene, Othello strangles Desdemona. In the article we read:

Sammie wanted the part, he explains, to make sure that when his character was tempted by violence, Sammie himself wouldn't be.

"In prison, it's like the alcoholic who says: 'I've been in for five years, and I haven't drunk for five years.' It's easy because you don't have access to it. Playing Othello and Proteus, that gave me access to it instantly. I wanted to challenge myself to make sure how would I respond."

Memories of his crime hit him in a rehearsal for *Othello*. Sammie started to sob.

"It really broke me down. ... . And what was really great was having all my partners there to support me. It's like getting down to the truth and delivering it."

Last year, Sammie got a letter whose return address bore the last name of a woman he'd slept with. It began, "Hi, my name is Desiree, and I am your daughter. I'm eighteen years old, and if you'd like to know me, please write me back." Sammie says of that moment, "I have never been happier in my life."[*]

The letter led to a moving reconciliation, to which Sammie's own reconciliation with himself through Shakespeare seems to have contributed a major role. In Desiree's second letter, his daughter wrote, "I've already forgiven you for not being there for me." Sammie stated, "I needed to hear that."

They met later in the year, and as Sammie relates, "We fell instantly in love, me and Desi. We write all the time."[**]

Exposure to Shakespeare's non-dramatic literature is also encouraged, and one of the prisoners committed Shakespeare's sonnets to memory to recite to his daughters when they visited. He stated, "They and Shakespeare are now my great loves."[***]

[*]*The Christian Science Monitor, A Guide to Education and Lifelong Learning.* July 27, 2004.
[**]Ibid.
[***]Ibid.

231

This following story took place during the 2000–2001 academic year, when I was conducting workshops with a group of incarcerated young men at the Pere Marquette Detention Center for teenage boys in Grafton, Illinois.

Meetings took place on Thursday evenings. Most of the group were from single family homes, and though there were a few whites, the majority were African-American and Hispanic. Most of the boys had gotten into trouble in large cities, principally Chicago. Many were picked up for drug trafficking and theft.

We were involved with writing poetry, and I invited anyone who wanted to read his poem to the rest of the group could do so. Poems like the following were presented:

I learned this just when I was a little child
Listen to what I am trying
To tell you
Think your friends are all
Ways trying to fail you.
That when you need a friend they are never around
They may act like and
Say they are going to do things,
But the time come they stay out in the rain.

I want to go home.
I want to use the phone
Because I feel so very alone.
You shouldn't have done wrong.
Home sweet home.

DOC* *has got me down.*
It's like my mind spinning around.
Up and down, round and round,
My head is spinning like a crazy clown.

One hot and windy day, the police came flying my way,
They asked me what I was doing here on this block.
I told them I didn't have nothing in my socks,
They took me to the police station and asked me a lot of
    questions.
They hit me twice for making the wrong suggestions.
So I'm telling you today,
Next time you see the police flying your way,
Say out loud and proud,
I didn't do it on a windy day.

I told them how good their poetry was, and then I asked if anyone would be interested in acting out any of the circumstances behind these poems? There was a pause. Then one boy said he would like to do that, then another, and that was enough to begin. I invited them and any others dramatize their stories in the next session.

One of the boys, Ramos, had a lot of pent-up anger. He resented any authority, and got angry when he felt he was being belittled. He had been expelled from the group for fighting two weeks before, and ordered into a state of isolation from the other boys.

I pleaded with the director of the facility to have him reinstated, explaining that what we were doing would help with the boy's problems of anger and rebellion, adding that Ramos needed the support of the group now more than ever. The director finally

*Department of Corrections

agreed to let him re-enter the group on the condition that there would be no more fighting. I assured him of this, and now Ramos was back.

I asked for volunteers. "Who would like to make a scene about their own lives?" Ramos lifted his arm in strong affirmation.

The exercise began. I first asked him a little bit about where he came from, and what his life had been like before coming to the detention center. He recounted a life with five siblings in a single family home in the outskirts of Chicago. The mother was tied up all day trying to care for her baby girl. They were living precariously in a one-room flat, for which they were being grossly overcharged, and living on food stamps. His brothers and sisters were too young to work and were trying to stay in school. Only Ramos, sixteen, was of working age, but he could not find a job. He was approached one day by a friend who was selling drugs and bringing in $300–$400 a week. Ramos proceeded to join the gang of drug providers. During the third night of passing crack, two Chicago cops pounced on him as he was closing a deal.

I asked Ramos if he would be willing to dramatize his arrest in a brief scene. He thought about how he was going to do this, and I told him I would help him create a scene. He signaled a hesitant "OK."

We set up a situation. He was to play himself, and two of his friends would take the parts of the police. He gave them instructions on the behavior of the cops, and the scene began.

Ramos was standing casually on a Chicago street corner, looking for a "buyer." After a few moments, the two boys enacting the policemen swooped down and grabbed him roughly by the arms. He was furious at being manhandled and kicked, pushed and swore. The authorities only got rougher, throwing him against a wall.

"We don't want to hurt you, but do you have any drugs?"

"None of your business, man."

"We'll make it our business if you don't hold still. Let me see what's in your pockets."

"No, man!"

Searching his pockets, the authorities located a small envelope. But the struggle continued.

"Come on, now, get into the car." (Three chairs has been set up, two front and one behind.) They threw Ramos into the back seat.

That was as far as we took the improvisation. In the action that followed, we learned that he put everybody on a short fuse at the station house as he defiantly lit a cigarette in the face of the booking officer.

"What did you think?" I asked the boys.

There was a pause. The boys seemed reluctant to criticize Ramos. But I explained that their reactions might help him. Curtis volunteered: "That was stupid! No wonder you get in trouble. You were just asking for trouble acting like that, man!"

"How many agree?" I asked. Several hands were raised.

"Could Ramos have acted differently." I asked. A pause.

"Yes," volunteered Pruitt. "He could have acted with respect. He didn't have any *respect*. He didn't need to get that angry."

"How many agree?"

The boys knew him well and had all been party to his anger.

After a pause, Felipe said, "Thass' right. You didn't need to act that way."

"What do you think, Ramos?" I asked. "Can you act without anger?"

"No, man. I get so furious. I always get angry when they tell me what to do."

"Do you think that your anger is helping or hurting you in these cases?"

"I dunno."

"I'm asking you to think."

Silence. Then one of the boys volunteered emphatically, "But that's what's causing you the trouble. If you had acted with respect you wouldn't be here."

This was a debatable point, but I wanted to see if Ramos might make the connection. "Do you think it's possible to break a habit like anger?" I asked.

Ramos paused and began to reflect. One could sense meaningful wheels turning within. But after several seconds he still murmured, "I dunno'."

A door was opening hesitantly.

"Would you be willing to try it?"

"Whaddya mean?"

"I mean try tonight, like right now."

"How can I do that?"

"Simple. You're a good actor. So let's play the scene again. Only this time, let's see if you can act your part but be respectful to the cops."

A skeptical frown.

"Why don't you *try*? Just to see what happens?"

Another pause, then "O.K. I'll try it."

We began the scene again. Ramos was seized by the officers, and though one could sense Mt. Etna threatening to erupt, the culprit managed to stand still.

He was asked if he had any crack.

The temptation toward defiance almost took over. But recalling his task, he replied respectfully, "Yes, sir, I have a little in an envelope."

The class fairly gasped.

"We have to search you."

"That won't be necessary, officer. Here," as a crumpled envelope was produced.

There was a burst of laughter. The boys had never seen this side of Ramos. And now Ramos began to relish his new role!

A co-operative Ramos now entered the squad car as the class cheered!

We invited Ramos to remain on stage for a discussion. He was clearly feeling triumphant. I couldn't help but marvel that here, in just these few minutes, we were seeing the muscles of change growing before our eyes. And I could only conjecture what might be achieved with Ramos and these boys if we could only carry on a longer program.

When I asked the group if the non-violent behavior of Ramos might help him in life, the boys universally replied, "Yeah, man." "No doubt."

"How did you feel the second time?" I asked Ramos.

"Well it was hard. When the cops grabbed me, it was hard."

"But you can do it, right?"

"Well maybe."

"But you just *did* it! You *showed* us all that you could do it!" I turned to the class, "Am I *crazy*, or didn't he just *do* it?"

Like a musical chorus, "Yeah, yeah, Ramos, *you did it!!!*"

There was a pause. Then he said, almost reluctantly, "Yeah, I guess I did it."

"And if you did it *here*, do you think that you could do it on the outside?"

"I don' know."

"How many of you think Ramos can do it outside?"

Another pause.

Then Curtis, a mild-mannered young boy, spoke for the first time and quietly uttered the words I shall never forget:

"I think ya' can do it, Ramos. But, Ramos, you gotta' *practice*."

THIRTEEN

KABUL, 1976: WINDOWS OF
JOY OPEN*

For centuries, art has always been well recognized as a means of uniting humankind. As international performing arts programs cross and re-cross our globe, we become increasingly aware of how hearts are touched, sometimes by the simplest performance events, enabling the bonding qualities of good will and affection to connect us.

Renowned theatre innovator and director Peter Brook observes that all that is needed to make theatre is an actor and an "empty space." And as Peter Schumann, the creator of the Bread and Puppet theatre has stated and demonstrated, that space can be anywhere, "the stairs, the windows, the streets, the doors."

This is the story of how the author found himself an accidental and living demonstration of these truths years ago.

It was 1976 and The Richard Morse Mime Theatre was performing in Kabul, Afghanistan. It was three years before the disastrous Russian invasion. On a fresh spring afternoon I wandered away from the city with no objective in mind except to explore the surroundings of the city. For about a half hour I ambled along a dirt

*Reprinted with permission of *The Christian Science Monitor.*

road that wound upward toward a wooded area. With the city a good distance behind me, I suddenly became aware of young voices chanting in the distance. "The Koran," I thought. "At last I'll hear it."

Continuing, I discerned a wooden schoolhouse through the trees. The school consisted of one room set upon a porch. A door frame had lost its door long ago, as had two window frames their windows. I peeked inside and saw a lightly bearded instructor in a worn blue suit and open-collared white shirt conducting some 20 boys in a recitation. They looked to be about thirteen or fourteen years of age. I approached gingerly to try to observe undetected through a small corner of the window. But all at once, the teacher turned his head toward my hiding place. Now we were staring at each other in mutual bewilderment. An embarrassed eavesdropper, I waved sheepishly and began to withdraw. But the teacher seemed to welcome the interruption, and eagerly beckoned me to enter the schoolroom.

I made my way up two sagging front steps. Now in the doorway, I pressed my palms together under my chin as I had seen them do in some film or other like *Lawrence of Arabia,* attempting a type of eastern salutation that might have found inclusion in one of those State Department manuals under the rubric of "*First step in making the right first impression in Afghanistan.*" The teacher smiled sympathetically. Now the teacher and I were viewing each other in a diffident curiosity.

"You are English?" the instructor asked.

"No. American," I replied with a tinge of temerity. In those days there was a considerable resentment toward the United States policies that supported the Shah in neighboring Iran.

"Oh," he said with astonishment. And again, "Oh."

There a pause of assessment. But he quickly added, "Excuse me. But we have never seen an American before."

The class looked on in wide-eyed fascination. "Where does he keep his gun?" I felt them wondering. "Or his horse."

"Are you from Texas?" the teacher asked.

"No, no. Far from Texas."

"Chicago?"

"No, I come from New York," I answered, dispelling one mystery, but potentially inviting another. "I come from New York, and I work in the theatre."

"Ahh!" he beamed. "You know Gary Cooper?"

"Not exactly," I replied. "America is very big."

"Ahh, yes," he said a bit disappointedly.

"We have a theatre company, and we are visiting your city of Kabul."

"Ah," he repeated. "And what do you do?"

"We are a mime theatre," I explained.

Total incomprehension. With words failing, I threw myself into a demonstration. "You see, like this." And I mimed opening an imaginary door and entering a room.

The children chuckled. Children are always quick to suggest the next move. I continued by climbing an imaginary staircase. The young Afghanis burst into gleeful laughter and applauded. There was a pause, and then, "Please, please, do one more," implored the instructor.

For my next "number," I placed my hands under two imaginary handles and, with some effort, slowly opened an invisible window. The window now open, I hunched down and leaned forward through the imaginary window space toward the class. Discovering the young Afghanis on the other side, I waved enthusiastically. A young boy in the third row returned my greeting. And now the entire class was giggling and waving wildly at their new friend. The classroom bubbled with mirth and cries of "Hello!" "Hello, sir!"

"More!" "More!" two or three cried.

We all grasped magical balloon strings. Presently, the skies over Kabul were filled with young Afghani children floating gently heavenward. We rose wondrously above the hilltops where we all swooped and gyrated balletically among flocks of astonished hawks and crows. Then we all descended and landed gently in the midst of the city's ancient vegetable market.

"That's good! That's very good!" exclaimed the teacher as he brushed his eyes with his sleeve. (He had flown with us.) "Chakeran," he said in Farsi. ("I am at your service.")

"Chakeran," I replied.

The excited murmuring of the class now subsiding, I mumbled some words to the teacher about not wishing to interrupt the lesson further. Waving to the boys, I called out using my limited vocabulary, "Chakeran! Chakeran!"

"Goodbye!" "Goodbye, sir!" "You come back!" they called in return.

At the doorway, I paused to wave farewell to the class. But a boy in the front of the class interrupted my intention, and rose from his chair. "Please!" he cried. Without warning, the boy placed his hands on two invisible window handles, and, struggling with considerable effort, he lifted the window frame over his head. Leaning his body forward, he waved to me calling, "Goodbye! Goodbye, sir!"

And now, one by one, all the children opened windows and waved their arms. "Goodbye!" "Goodbye, sir!" "Goodbye, friend!"

Now, many years later, with so many windows of the world demolished by acts of violence, my mind often returns to my young friends. What has become of them? I wonder. And their kind teacher? Is the little schoolhouse still there?

If many windows of the world seem recently to have been shattered, we can always look through others that wait only to be opened.

FOURTEEN

A SUMMARY

The French equivalent of the English phrase "to raise a child" is "*élever un enfant.*" Webster defines the word, "elevate," in part, as "to lift or raise from a lower to a higher place." Deconstructing the word further, we trace its origins to its original Latin root, "*elevare,*" a compound of "e"- "out of" and "levis," -or "light," in the sense of lightening a burden. This is one of many examples where translations can provide interesting insights.

The French phrase "*élever un enfant*" might well define the process of teaching. In the course of "lightening" heavy burdens, we free our children to rise to new plateaus of hope and possibility.

To recapitulate what we have witnessed: In Part One, Lucia Lopez is lifted from a lifetime of violence through participation in a theatre group; young displaced Korean immigrant, Han, is removed from a vacuum of loneliness to discover a new family; a five-year-old deaf Bolivian child, Gueddy, leaps impetuously onto the stage in a life-changing moment which leads him to transcend his disability and inspire thousands in South and North America; Bronx ninth-grader, Geoffrey, is lifted triumphantly onto the shoulders of his supporting classmates as he rises above suicidal tendencies; and through this same theatre program, veteran teacher Miriam Sokol of Pablo Casals Public School 181, witnesses her school year rise from a dispiriting dreariness to become, in the words of this delighted teacher, "a howling success—the highlight of my teaching career."

In Part Two, we observe revolutionary educators, Rousseau,

Pestalozzi and Froebel, fighting to lift the intolerably heavy atmosphere of the classroom to one of play and collaboration. The first to employ theatre methods in the schools, Harriet Finlay Johnson, sees her students so filled with the joy of learning that they cannot be kept from the classroom; H. Caldwell Cook releases the inherent power of students to soar to Shakespearean heights, once given credit for their abilities to learn; and Peter Slade helps thousands to rediscover healing spontaneity through exhilarating improvisations and is crowned as the undisputed "father of drama therapy."

Modern teachers build on these discoveries. Meade Palidofsky removes the burdens of hopelessness from the shoulders of her young prisoners and they write moving poetry and plays; David Booth frees the downtrodden vision of children and leads them to contemplate "sand castles" within; Sherry and Bob Jason take thousands of young people imprisoned by squalid street conditions of Skid Row, to where their bodies take flight in the ballet studio; Sunna Rasch's young casts "hold the mirror up to nature" and help lift the yoke of drug addiction from the shoulders of thousands; David Willingham releases the hidden powers of music in transforming street youth who develop new "intelligences before his eyes," and Gus Rogerson lifts his young students from the pot-holed streets of New York's Hell's Kitchen to sun-drenched country fields where their imaginations leap to vibrant life in the creation of beautiful plays.

In Part Three we see how past theatre practice can enrich the present. Ancient traditions of shamanism, masks and clowning reveal the healing powers of 'inclusion' that ripple through classrooms, hospitals, and prisons throughout the world. Emboldened by the *Commedia* mask, shy Laure Anne becomes a raging tower of strength; the incarcerated Ramos, supported by fellow inmates, discovers that he has the strength to conquer violence. Costumed in outlandish clown motley, and bearing only wide grins and bags

243

full of toys, the clowns of Patch Adams lift the spirits of orphaned, hospitalized, and incarcerated children in all corners of the world.

What a legacy these leaders have provided for us, weaving unforgettable connections through story, dance, mime, and clowning! They echo the sentiments of Rousseau:

> *"Give the child something to be enthused about, point the child in the right direction, and what will not the child achieve?"*

With a little boost from us, our children *can* re-open the windows to a different world, where separation, frustration and violence are replaced by connection, self-esteem and the celebration of family.

BIBLIOGRAPHY

John Allen, *Drama in Schools: its Theory and Practice.* Heinemann Publishers, Portsmouth, N.H., 1979.

Alexander W. Astin, *Preventing Students from Dropping Out.* Jossey-Bass Publishers, San Francisco, 1975.

Aristotle's Theory of Poetry and Fine Art. (Trans. S.H. Butcher.) Dover Publications, New York, 1951.

D. A. Beacock, *Play Way English for To-day: The Methods and Influence of H. Caldwell Cook.* Thomas Nelson and Sons Ltd, London, 1943.

Robert Bly, *The Sibling Society.* Vintage Books, New York, 1977.

Gavin Bolton, *Acting in Classroom Drama.* Calendar Islands Publishers, Portland, Maine, 1999.

Augusto Boal, *Theatre of the Oppressed.* (Trans. Charles A. and Maria Leal McBride.) Theatre Communications Group, New York, 1985.

Mary Bowmaker, *A Little School on the Downs: The story of pioneer educationalist Harriet Finlay Johnson, headmistress at Sompting School, West Sussex, 1897–1910.* Woodfield Publishing, Bognor Regis, 2002.

Ernest L. Boyer, *High School: A Report on Secondary Education in America.* Harper & Row Publishers, New York, 1983.

Oscar G. Brockett, *History of the Theatre.* Allyn & Bacon Inc., Boston, 1987.

Joseph Campbell, *The Hero with a Thousand Faces.* Princeton University Press, 1949.

———, *Myths to Live By.* Penguin Group, New York, 1972.

———, *The Power of Myth,* with Bill Moyers. Doubleday, New York, 1988.

Richard Courtney, *Play, Drama and Thought: the Intellectual Background to Dramatic Education.* Simon & Pierre, Toronto, 1989.

Lawrence A. Cremin, *Traditions of American Education.* Basic Books Inc., New York, 1977.

John Dewey, *Democracy and Education.* The MacMillan Co., New York, 1916.

————, *Lectures in China, 1919–1920.* An East-West Center Book, The University Press of Hawaii, 1973.

————, *The Quest for Certainty.* Capricorn Books, G.P. Putnam's Sons, 1929.

————, *The Theory of the Moral Life.* Holt, Rinehart and Winston, 1908.

————, *Philosophy of Education.* Littlefield, Adams & Co., 1958.

Alan Elsner, *Gates of Injustice: The Crisis in America's Prisons.* Prentice Hall, Upper Saddle River, New Jersey, 2004.

Frederich Froebel, *The Education of Man.* (Trans. W. M. Hallman.) Appleton and Co., New York, 1887.

William Glasser, *The Quality School; Managing Students Without Coercion.* Harper Collins Books, New York, 1990.

Roger Grainger, *Drama and Healing: The Roots of Drama Therapy.* Jessica Kingsley Publishers, London, 1995.

Ronald Gross, Editor, *The Teacher and the Taught: Education in Theory and Practice from Plato to James B. Conant.* Delta Books, 1963.

Ronald Gottesman, Editor in Chief, Richard Maxwell Brown, Consulting Editor, *Violence in America, An Encyclopedia.* Scribners and Sons, New York, 1999.

Maxine Greene, *Releasing the Imagination: Essays on Education, the Arts, and Social Change.* Jossey-Bass Publishers, San Francisco, 1995.

Dorothy Heathcote and Gavin Bolton, *Drama for Learning, Dorothy Heathcote's Mantle of the Expert Approach to Education.* Heinemann, 1994.

Oscar Handlin, *John Dewey's Challenge to Education.* Harper and Brothers, New York, 1959.

Larry A. Hickman and Thomas M. Alexander, Editors, *The Essential Dewey.* Indiana University Press, Bloomington and Indianapolis, 1998.

Sue Jennings, Editor, *Dramatherapy: Theory and Practice for Teachers and Clinicians.* Croom Helm. London and Sydney, 1987.

———, *Dramatherapy: Theory and Practice 2.* Tavistock/Routledge, London and New York, 1992.

Sue Jennings and Ase Minde, *Art Therapy and Dramatherapy: Masks of the Soul.* Jessica Kingsley Publishers, London, 1993.

Harriet Finlay Johnson, *The Dramatic Method of Teaching.* James Nisbet and Co., London, n.d.

Dorothy Heathcote and Gavin Bolton, *Drama for Learning.* Heinemann, Portsmouth, N.H., 1994.

Grady Hillman, *Arts Programs for Juvenile Offenders in Detention Centers and Corrections.* The National Endowment for the Arts, 1999.

John H. Hunley, *Masks: Faces of Culture.* Harry N. Abrams, Inc., New York, 2002.

Jonathan Kozol, *Amazing Grace: The Lives of Children and the Conscience of a Nation.* Crown Publishers, New York, 1995.

———, *Savage Inequalities: Children in America's Schools,* Harper Perennial, New York, 1991.

Jonathan Levy, *A Theatre of the Imagination: Reflections on Children and the Theatre.* New Plays Inc., Charlottesville, VA, 1987.

Gary O. Larson, *American Canvas: An Arts Legacy for Our Communities.* National Endowment for the Arts, 1997.

Hughes Mearns, *Creative Power: The Education of Youth in the Creative Arts.* Dover Publications, Inc., New York, 1958.

Metropolitan Life Survey of the American Teacher 1994: Violence in America's Public Schools: The Family Perspective. Louis Harris and Associates, New York, 1994.

James Moffett, *The Universal Schoolhouse: Spiritual Awakening through Education.* Calendar Island Publishers, Portland, Maine, 1998.

Patricia Montoya, Commissioner, *Child Maltreatment 1997.* U. S. Department of Health and Human Services, 1997.

Cecily O'Neil and Alan Lambert, *Drama Structures: A Practical Handbook for Teachers.* Heinemann, Portsmouth, N.H., 1982.

Jenny Pearson, Editor, *Discovering the Self through Drama and Movement: The Sesame Approach,* Jessica Kingsley Publishers, London, 1996.

Plato, *Gorgias*. (Trans. W. C. Helmbold.) The Bobbs Merrill Co. Publishers, 1952.

Plato, *Great Dialogues of Plato*. (Trans. W. H. D. Rouse.) A Mentor Book, New American Library, New York and Toronto, 1956.

Neil Postman, *Amusing Ourselves to Death*. Viking Penguin, Inc., New York, 1965.

———, *The Disappearance of Childhood*. Vintage Books, New York, 1982.

———, *Technopoly*. Vintage Books, New York, 1983.

———, *Building a Bridge to the Eighteenth Century*. Alfred A. Knopf, New York, 1999.

Jean Jacques Rousseau, *Émile, ou l'Education*. (Trans. Barbara Boxley.) Everyman's Library, London, 1911.

———, *The Émile, of Jean Jacques Rousseau* (Trans. and ed. by William Boyd.) Heinneman, London, 1956.

Paul Arthur Schlipp, Editor, *The Philosophy of John Dewey*. Northwestern University, Evanston and Chicago, 1939.

Ronald L. Simon and Marc Estrin, *Rehearsing with Gods: Photographs and Essays on the Bread and Puppet Theater*. Chelsea Green Publishing Company, White River Junction, Vermont, 2004.

Peter Slade, *Child Drama and its Value in Education: Address given at the 1st Drama Conference of the Department of Education and Science for Wales*. Bangor University, April, 1965.

———, *Experience of Spontaneity*, Longmans Press, London and Harlow, 1968.

Jean Trounstine, *Shakespeare Behind Bars*. The University of Michigan Press, Ann Arbor, 2001.

U. S. Department of Health and Human Services, *12 Years of Reporting Child Maltreatment*. Government Printing Office, Washington, D.C., 2001.

U.S. Department of Justice, Federal Bureau of Investigation, *Crime in the United States*. Washington, D.C., 1999.

J. Michael Walton, *Tragedy Reviewed: The Greek Sense of Theatre*. Methuen, London and New York, 1984.

Betty Jane Wagner and Dorothy Heathcote, *Drama as a Learning Medium*. Calendar Islands Publishers, Portland, Maine, 1976.

Pat Watts, essay in *Drama Therapy and Practice*, 2. (Ed. by Sue Jennings.) Tavistock, Routledge, London, New York, 1992.

Media: newspapers, pamphlets, brochures

John Cloud, "The Legacy of Columbine." *Time Magazine,* 33–35, March 19, 2001.

Bernardine Dohrn, "Youth violence: false fears and hard truths." *Educational Leadership*, vol. 55, 2–5, Oct. 1997.

Steven Durland, "Maintaining Humanity: Grady Hillman talks about arts programs in correctional setting." *Art in the Public Interest*, 1996.

James L. Jarrett, "Values through the Arts." *Art Education,* March, 1981.

William Donald Schaefer, *Governor's Report.* Annapolis, MD, 1994.

Judith Humphreys Weitz, *Coming Up Taller: Arts and Humanities Programs for Children at Risk.* President's Committee on the Arts and the Humanities, 1996.

The National Endowment for the Arts, *Eloquent Evidence: Arts at the Core of Learning.* Oct. 1995.

———, *The Arts and Education: Partners in Achieving Our National Goals.* 1995.

Arts Education Partnership Working Group, *The Power of the Arts to Transform Education.* Kennedy Center, Washington, D.C.

Mary Wittenberg, "Acting with Conviction." *The Christian Science Monitor,* Learning Section: 11–18, July 24, 2001.

New York Times. Butterfield Fox, "Study Tracks Boom in Prisons and Notes Impact on Counties." April 30, 2004.

———. Ford Fessenden, "They Threaten, They Seethe and Unhinge, Then Kill in Quantity." p. 1, 20. April 9, 2000.

———. Robert D. McFadden, "Violence, Real and Imagined, Sweeps Through the Schools." 1A, p. 26. April 30, 1999.

———. Emily Yellin, *As Jonesboro Shooting Fades, A Killer's Family Still Lives It.* p.1. April 27, 1999.

———. Erica Goode. "Deeper Truths Sought in Violence by Youths." p. 24. April 30, 1999.

————. "Columbine Students Talk of the Disaster and Life." A5. April 30, 1999.

————. "The Eight Who Shared Feelings and Opinions." A25. April 30, 1999.

————. Adrian Nicole LeBlanc, "The Outsiders." Magazine Section, p. 36–41. August 23, 1999

St. Louis Post Dispatch. "Students blame bullying, victimizing and failing to communicate for the violence in our schools." Articles by Allison Keely, Amanda Austermann, Rusty Michener, B1. August 29, 1999.

Beth Murray, Ph.D. dissertation, *Nowhere to Hide But Together.* 1998.

ABOUT THE AUTHOR

Richard Morse's career has spanned almost six decades, including work as an actor, mime artist, director and teacher in New York, regional theatre and abroad.

The Richard Morse Mime Theatre made its debut at the Cleveland Play House, in the 1971–1972 season, where, with Richard's original partner, Pilar Garcia, it was an overwhelming success. Three concert performances featuring Mr. Morse as soloist with the Cleveland Orchestra followed.

September 11, 1977 was proclaimed *Richard Morse Mime Theatre Day* by New York's Mayor Edward Koch on the occasion of the troupe's fifth anniversary performance at Lincoln Center. The award recognized both the company's high level of artistry and its provision of live theatre for many economically and physically disadvantaged audiences in New York's five boroughs.

Morse Mime has now been acclaimed in 26 countries, including on three U.S. State Department tours.

Mr. Morse taught mime, acting, theatre styles and musical theatre from 1961 through 1988 at New York's HB (Uta Hagen—Herbert Berghof) Studio, and 1973–1982 at his own Morse Mime Academy. He has also been a guest teacher at the New York University Graduate School of Theatre, the American Academy of Dramatic Arts, and New York's Neighborhood Playhouse. From 1988 to 1999 Mr. Morse was Professor of Theatre at Principia College.

Richard now makes his home in southern Illinois overlooking the Mississippi River with his wife, Bente, and their two dogs.